# Last *of the*

# English

# Roses

**Charlotte Kendrick**

Shrubs Publishing

*To the people of Britain,*

*After several visits to England and forming cherished friendships
with remarkable Brits, I began to hear stories about World War
II that deeply impacted me. The conditions they endured, shared
with me with unwavering resilience and charm, left an indelible
impression. It became clear that I needed to write about it.*


*With profound appreciation for your history and your enduring
spirit, I dedicate this book to you. Your stories have touched me
deeply, and I hope these pages reflect the unwavering courage
and strength you have displayed in the face of adversity.*

# Last *of the* English Roses

# *Chapter One*

The warm May sun pushed through the lush greenery of the secluded Rose family cemetery after a light misty rain. The scent of spring revealed the renewal of the earth coming out of its hibernation.

Elizabeth and Alicia Rose stood mesmerized in front of the mountain of flowers on the gray metallic casket that held the remains of their father who died from an illness he had struggled with for the past ten years.

Anticipating his death at anytime the two sisters did their best to please their father in any way they could and wanted his last days to be the best possible under the distressing circumstances and his wishes were customarily fulfilled. Their lives were centered on him, and now he was gone.

Their feelings at that moment were ambiguous. The freedom from Creighton William Rose's demanding grasp upon them, and the emptiness of his passing.

The other members of the family and assorted friends were starting to wander off after quietly making their sympathies known to the two sisters.

"Are we ready to go home? The grounds men are pacing and wanting to lower the casket as soon as we leave.

I want to take some flowers to dry for my journal Elizabeth whispered to her sister who was ten years younger, as they slowly walked to the mound of flowers. "

"Yes, I'm ready and I want to take some too. What time is the reception?" Alicia asked.

"Not until four o'clock. We have plenty of time. Please stay in your dress. Wait until after the reception to change into your casual clothes." Elizabeth said changing her demeanor.

"Oh, alright, you always were a spoilsport. I will do as you say your majesty. I guess you're the boss now that father is gone."

"What makes you say that? I have never bossed you in my life."

Elizabeth protested as they walked to the waiting long black limousine.

"Spoil sport. I am sorry if I am little 'lisha'...but now that father is gone, I can say anything I please. I remember many times I would have liked to have put a restraint on your perfect little world and make you behave. "Elizabeth confronted her sister, for the first time allowing her jealousy towards her, to come out into the open.

2

"That's not true. I did *not* live in a perfect world. I had to obey him too." Alicia said as she plunged into the car.

"You most certainly did not. You could do anything. It always amazed me just how far you could go without father getting upset with you. You constantly got by with everything."

Each sister took a deep breath to calm down and each sat silent for the rest of the drive to 'Roselyn', the Rose estate located a few kilometers north of London.

The grandeur of the Roselyn estate radiated its beauty in the sunlight as they passed through the old Iron Gate, which had been modernized with computerized security that would open with the swipe of a card.

Generations of the Rose family grew up with in its walls and had endured many things throughout the years. The grand old gray stone manor with glistening black paned windows was embellished with cries, whispers, love, hate and anger of the beautiful ones and the homely ones, the old ones the young ones, the mothers, fathers, brothers, sisters. Many tear-stained walls marked each generation with their sorrows and many walls of happiness.

Today would be the start of a new history for the family estate and trust, with one generation passing with another's beginning. Time would only tell if this new era would be a happy one or full of grief and misery as the last one had been.

The long black car wound around the extended curved drive way that led to the manor. The sun immersed the palatial estate with warm light allowing it to radiate its antiquated grandeur and beauty that had been seasoned by the Rose family.

"Will you need me anymore today?" The chauffeur asked the reticent siblings.

"No, thank you Travis, we will be in the rest of the day. The reception for father is at four o'clock."

Their butler Hodges, who had been with the family for many years, greeted them. He was the son of the previous butler and was prepared for the job from his youth. He enjoyed his job as had his father.

The massive entryway with its large black and white checkered tiles didn't seem as inviting as it had before the funeral. Something definitely was missing. The absence of their father who had ruled the large estate all their lives could be felt. It was a daunting feeling knowing they would not have to run up the stairs to his room to see what his needs were and then she would be controlled by him.

They leisurely started up the extended winding staircase with the sun streaming through the antique black paned windows trying to add brightness to their dreary day.

"I'm sorry I spoke so rudely to you just now in the car. I guess I am just at a loss without father. It is going to be so strange without him. It is going to be so quiet without his shouting at us. Are you feeling this too?"

"Yes, I suppose so. I never thought about feeling a need for him to yell at us though, the house would always be in an uproar when he did that."

"Just the power in his voice alone could fill the walls, then at the end he was so weak. I felt so sorry for him losing his vigor. His masculinity disappeared into a fragile little man. I want to remember him as a strong man. The sense of humor though sarcastic he could have at times that made me laugh. I want to forget his growing demands especially in his later years. I want to forget all the negative things about him, don't you?"

"I suppose. Is that healthy to do that, to deliberately deny he was such a mean old man at the end?" Alicia asked.

"Of course, we just need to acknowledge that sometimes elderly people get senile and that is what I'm going to forget and keep in mind only the good parts of our life with him. That *is* healthy and will be *the* way I am going to cope with the future without him. I hope you will too. I don't want to share anything bad about him with anyone other than you if the occasion should ever arise. I can't see why it would serve any purpose to scrutinize our daily life we had with him to anyone."

"My dominating bad memory is the Rose line stopped with him. He could never accept not having a son to continue his name. He seethed at the thought his younger brother, Timothy had a son. Then to make things even worse moved to America. It did haunt him didn't it Lizzy?"

"Yes, Lisha, it did. He was such a brilliant man, and hardworking but he didn't have control over not having a son to bear his name. I remember nights only lately he would bring the subject up…" if only'," he would whisper…" if only I had a son."

"How did that make you feel? I always felt like apologizing to him everyday of my life for that error of mother nature that *I* wasn't born a boy."

"Me too. I think that is one thing we will never forget and can be added to the list of things not necessary to talk about any longer there is no need is there?"

"No, not really, I still have the feelings of inadequacy and never measuring up."

"I wonder how Timothy and his children are doing. Father said he was struggling and his business in America was not doing so well. That was, several years ago he even brought his name up. I do have his address. I want to find out how they are. I'd like to see them, wouldn't you?"

"Yes, I would. I thought about that too. We will contact them."

"Now, baby sister, you have your wedding to look forward to. Have you set the date?"

"Now see that is another matter, I had to wait for father to die before I could get married. He wouldn't ever let me talk about Jordan. When I tried to, he would interrupt me and change the subject. No, we haven't set the date but will soon. We just want to start our life and have lots of children. Both boys and *girls*." She said giving her sister a peck oh the cheek.

"What was that for?"

"That my big 'sis', is for being the best sister and friend a girl could ever have. I truly mean that, even though there are times....' Her voice trailed off as each sister entered her bedroom.

# Chapter Two

The morning rain gently palpated the bedroom windows making it known it would be a day for umbrellas and hats, which would be a very fitting day for Elizabeth's melancholy mood.

Stretching and yawning she slowly raised from her oversized bed handed down to her from her grandmother Rose, who always told her that since she was the oldest grandchild, she was to inherit *all* her possessions when she died. Elizabeth did not really care at the time her grandmother had shared that with her when she just a young girl, but now it was important to her and she now appreciated the sentiment and inheritance.

Their ancestors' generations ago stated that the oldest male was always the heir, and if there were no male heirs, the oldest female would inherit everything. Now she was feeling the heavy mantel of such a large family trust. What would she do?

Only now she could truly understand how her father felt before he died. No male heirs. No one to carry on the family name.

She crawled back under the warm cozy covers and rang for Beatrice to come start a fire for her in the old brick fireplace. Maybe that would cheer her up she thought, looking out at the dreary gray sky.

"Miss Elizabeth, may I come in?"

"Yes, Bea, please. Will you build a fire for me? I'm lazy this morning and hoped the warmth of a nice fire might perk me up."

"Of course, may I bring you a breakfast tray when I finish?"

"That would be wonderful. Thank you. What would I do without you? Isn't it quiet and peaceful? I am still waiting for father to call for me any moment but then I remember he is never going to call again." She started to cry.

"I'm so sorry Miss Elizabeth. Is there anything we can do to help you? It will take some time for you to get used to his absence. Until then you just remember we are here and will do anything for you that we can." Bea said softly holding her.

"How sweet you are. What a kind and generous thing to say. I will keep it in mind. Thank you I will need your support. I can tell this is going to take longer than I thought. I'm surprised how lifeless I feel."

"Do we need to phone the doctor? Are you sleeping soundly?"

"No, I'm not very much, only in sporadic naps. How did you know?"

"I went through this when my mother passed away when I was a child. I couldn't sleep and it took such a long time for me to overcome her death. I know all about what you are going through. Don't hesitate to ask for anything, even if you feel timid about it. I am here and the rest of the staff is as well. They all told me to tell you that. You are not alone. We are here to help in any way we can. You just ring anytime day or night."

"You are wonderful. Tell them for me I will definitely call them when and if I need them as well as you. Thank them for me, will you?"

"Of course, I will. Is there anything else? The fire is going well enough. I will be back shortly with your tray."

The glowing fire did slightly ease the dark mood she was in. Her lack of energy and depressive feelings were much stronger than she ever imagined it would be in the process of her mourning.

Just knowing the staff of servants in the house wanted to help her with her grief was a pleasant thought, and helped her feel not quite so alone.

Alicia was hardly around since the funeral. She and Jordan, her finance' were planning their wedding that would take place in two weeks so she was no help with her older sister's recovery.

"Thank you, Bea, for the tray, I'm just going to read today. With the rain, I don't' feel like going outside. I will have my dinner tray about six o'clock. Tell Mrs. Waverly I'll only have soup and a roll with a salad. She knows my favorite."

"What about lunch? You will need a lunch."

"No, I'm not really hungry. Just a light dinner, that's all, Bea, thank you."

The rain was not going to end soon she could tell by its insistent sound. This would be a perfect day to read and rest. No interruptions. No interference. She would catch up on her reading. She would be able to enjoy the books she'd had for some time but found she was not able to concentrate until now.

Soon though she found thoughts about her father interrupted any focus on her book, so Elizabeth finally laid it down and tried to go back to sleep, but she couldn't turn off the thoughts that poured into her mind.

She finally had to phone the doctor to come give her something so she could sleep.

"Elizabeth, Elizabeth. Wake up. What are you doing still in bed?" Alicia asked.

"Why, what time is it? What day is it?"

"What do you mean, what day is it?"

"I've been tired so I decided to sleep until the rain stopped."

"My darling sister, the rain stopped day before yesterday."

"What? Day before yesterday? How could I sleep so long?"

"I don't know. Beatrice phoned me and told me she couldn't wake you. The doctor came in, do you remember?"

"The doctor, Doctor Bernard was here, in my bedroom?"

"Yes, he was. Don't you remember you phoned him and he gave you a sedative because you couldn't sleep?"

"Vaguely, I guess I do now. This is incredible. I guess I *was* tired, no wonder I slept so well."

"I guess you did, you just slept two days."

"I will feel great now. I just need a long hot shower and off I go."

"Great. Now where are you going after your shower?"

"I don't know, I guess the garden. I need to see what the rain did to my roses and what they need. Cranston will help

12

me. I'll call him to go with me all around to be sure they are alright."

"Good idea, I have to go now, Jordan and I have some plans to make. You know the wedding is in two weeks?"

"Yes, I think I remember..."

"Good, you remember you said you would be my bride's maid?"

"You asked me when? I don't remember, but I will be honored to be your bridesmaid, thank you. I will look forward to it."

"Elizabeth, you sound strange, are you alright?"

"I'm fine, just need a shower. Go, do your wedding plans. See you soon."

Alicia went downstairs to talk to Beatrice, Elizabeth's personal maid, and Miss Pendle, the head of the housekeeping staff, and Mrs. Waverly, the cook, about keeping a close watch on her sister and to call Dr. Bernard anytime they thought she was not acting normal. To take turns watching her all day and night and phone her if they needed anything, she would be at Jordan's family estate that was several kilometers away from Roselyn.

"I'm sorry I can't be here with Elizabeth, but we are in the middle of our wedding plans and I have to have my gown made which will take several fittings. I know this is a lot to ask of you all, but please know I will compensate you all for your vigil. I am going to phone some of her university friends. She would be happy to see them, I think. At least it will be a start to get her out of the doldrums."

"We will be here and she will be under our care twenty-four hours a day. You don't have to worry about anything. We know your wedding plans will take up your most of your time and you cannot be here. Just don't worry and yes, having her friends come and go will be a source of healing for her. That is a very good idea."

"Thank you, hope it will help. Be sure you tell everyone that you are all invited to the wedding and the invitations are in the mail to each one of you and we want to see you all there."

"We will certainly be there and thank you for the invitation."

"Goodbye for now and you have the numbers for both Jordan and I. Keep me updated on her, I want to know how she is doing, she doesn't sound like her old self."

"Don't worry, we will."

The hot water was refreshing but it was not enough to help her overcome the uneasy feelings regarding sleeping for two days, and barely remembering Dr. Bernard's visit to give her a sedative to help her sleep.

Remembering she told Bea about her sleep was only in short intervals, nothing restful. Bea must have phoned him she knew she hadn't, that much she *could* remember.

Elizabeth was tall and carried herself smoothly and gracefully. Her light brown hair was streaked with blonde that highlighted her beautiful porcelain face and bright blue eyes.

She thought once again about her plan to check the roses she had been neglecting. This was the first time in years she had not taken extra good care of them. They were her source of accomplishment when she saw them grow from their budding stage and then she would tenderly help them mature into their splendid fully grown beauty.

The day passed slowly. The only member of the Rose family that remained on the estate was experiencing loneliness never anticipated before. She hadn't anticipated just how alone she would feel after her father was gone and that Alicia wouldn't be there any more, only short visits from now on.

The silence was too hard to bear. What could she do to make her life normal and happy? What could she do? She was cut off from everyone from her past. Her friends had almost all married and moved away. She hadn't kept up with any of them. Maybe it was time she tried to connect with them again. She could get her attorney to help her find them, at least her favorite ones, Beth and Zoë. Beth had been such a solid friend. Nothing wavering about her. She would always come through. She could always rely on her for anything.

Zoë, on the other hand was an airhead but, was a loyal and sweet friend that kept her and Beth laughing from her consistent innocent *inability* to 'catch on' to many of their discussions. The other two friends found themselves attempting to explain many things that just didn't make sense to her. She was also a good friend, just not the strong and perceptive person Beth had been.

Their times together at Cambridge were filled with struggles in their classes, Elizabeth's art history classes especially, yet they managed to find enjoyment there. Yes, she thought, what would I have done without them? I need to find out where they are what they are doing.

# *Chapter Three*

The bright ample kitchen, Mrs. Waverly had helped design in a remodel several years before, was filled with delicious aromas of her cakes, cookies and cream pies.

Her choices of orange, blue, yellow, green, and purple added colorful touches to the updated bricked wall ovens that were made for a comfortable level so she wouldn't have to bend over when placing the heavy pans of food in them.

Mr. Rose had given her total freedom in her choices of colors and the need she would have for any and all appliances that she wanted and to have them arranged any way she liked. The kitchen was hers to do as she pleased. He didn't care as long as she kept the meals going the way he liked them and when he wanted them. The kitchen worked out perfectly for both of them.

"Mrs. Waverly, do you have some time now for a staff meeting? Miss Pendle asked.

"Yes, I do. You want to meet here at the table?"

"That would be a good place. I just wanted to talk with everyone about Miss Elizabeth I am still concerned about her. She looks pale and thin. Don't you think?" Miss Pendle asked as they all sat around the large table.

"I do too. Maybe we can help her through this sad time."

"I just don't know what we can do to help her. This is something she will have to work through for herself. All I can see we could possibly do is check on her all day and night to make sure she is alright. Who has any ideas?" Beatrice asked the concerned staff.

"I don't know either. All she does is mope around the garden for a short time, then returns to her room. It breaks my heart to see her this way. She has lost her smile and she looks awful. Her hair is really in need of something. A hair dresser might come here. Do you think? Do you know who she goes to?" Mrs. Waverly asked.

"No, I sure don't." Travis the laconic chauffer groaned.

"Don't get me involved with your little schemes. I want no part of them. They'll backfire and you'll be sorry you interfered."

"Oh, don't be silly. What could happen? She could just say that she doesn't want her hair done. There is no harm in that." Beatrice said.

"She needs more than her hair done. I think she needs to go to a psychologist. I think she is so depressed she can't function. My brother went through a traumatic divorce and he had to go to one. It really helped him. Now he's leading a normal life. There for a while he could hardly get out of bed. "

"How on earth could we manage that? Maybe, I know let's call Alicia and ask her. I think she will agree something needs to be done before this goes on any longer. I'm going to phone her now." Hodges said getting up from the table.

"Sounds good to me too. She would be the one to actually be able to get anything done. We don't have any say in matters as personal as this." Beatrice said wanting to do anything to help Elizabeth.

Hodges returned with a smile. Alicia is coming over to check on her sister. I told her we were all worried about Elizabeth. She has been so busy with the wedding she hasn't had a chance to come over but will be here shortly, hopefully tonight or tomorrow."

"Good. I feel better, did you tell her about your brother?" Mrs. Waverly asked.

"Yes, I did. She was a little upset about that part of it. But I told her that her sister was acting the very same way my brother did after his divorce. She started to see what I was talking about. Guess she didn't want to believe Elizabeth could be that unhappy, but we have nothing to worry about as long as we get help if she gets too of situations. Those doctors are put here to help us. She needs help, and we will see she does not go into a decline."

"Good for you Hodges for having the courage to say that to Alicia. I do not know if I would have been able to do that, thank you I know she needed to hear your story about your brother. "Miss Pendle said.

"Yeah, it is a good thing, sorry I was so negative about the whole helping thing, but I'm not much good when it comes to helping someone. It usually does backfire on me when I have tried in the past. Maybe I won't totally give up on an open mind and give it another try when and if the circumstances should arise." Travis added.

"Now, I have tea and cakes for everyone. We can relax now and think of some little ways we can cheer Miss Elizabeth. You know like, little notes of 'Roses are red violets are blue, I love cookies and now you do too.' Then I can put cookies in a cute basket for her outside her door to surprise her." Mrs. Waverly said.

"I could say 'Roses are red and violets are blue and are here in this basket that I picked just for you.' "Cranston the gardener said laughing at his little impromptu poem.

21

"Let's see, I could say…Humm…what could I say? *'Roses are red, violets are blue, that has nothing to do with me, but I am here for you.'* I could put that note in a basket of chocolates she likes. I know which ones to get . That's what I am going to do." Travis shared with them his part of cheering her up.

"I could say… *'Roses are red, violets are blue, I am always here for you.'* I will put that note in the book I know she wants. Miss Pendle said satisfied with her contribution.

"I will say *'Roses are red and violets are blue, I love this movie and I know you do too.'* I heard her tell Alicia the other day the one she wanted. I will get it today and put it in a basket." Beatrice said also satisfied with her contribution.

The servants ate their cakes and drank their tea feeling much better about their 'oldest little rose', as they called her when no one else was around.

Alicia pulled into the driveway in her small red sports car that was given to her on her birthday by her father when he was still living a normal life a few years earlier. It made her so happy to have her own car, and not have to be driven everywhere in that big black car that took up so much room and was nothing but a bother to do the smallest errands.

Elizabeth had never learned how to drive. She was afraid to even try. It was quite another story for *her* to have

22

a car.  Her father didn't think she could handle the stress of all the traffic. He had wanted her to be driven. To keep her safe, but the truth was he needed to keep her under his control. If she were driving her own car she could get too independent. She was unaware of his reasoning in the driving matter. He had to keep one daughter close to him. He knew the younger one had too much exuberance and strength of character for him try to have power over but no so with the older one.  He manipulated her very easily and he assumed his control, took full advantage of her timidity, and kept her close to him.

"Elizabeth, are you here?"  Alicia asked tapping on her door.

"Yes, come in. I was just going to get up and…."

"You're still in bed?  It's almost seven o'clock in the evening."

"I know, I know.  I was just resting for a while. I've been tired lately. I'll be all right tomorrow."

"Let's get Bea to bring us a pot of tea, some of those little sandwiches and cakes Mrs. Waverly makes and have a good ole talk. Maybe one of the last long ones we can have before I get married. What do you say?"

"Ok, I'll take a quick shower, you ring Mrs. Waverly."

The sisters proceeded to relax on the large bed puffing up pillows and getting comfortable for a long 'girly talk' , after Beatrice brought the pair a large tray with mounds of sandwiches, chips, cakes and cookies and a large decanter of their favorite tea.

"I am worried about you Lizzie. You have to get yourself out of this depression. It's not only me that is worried. The whole house is concerned about your state of mind. They filled me in on your daily routine. Or rather lack of one. Talk to me and get it all out. Tell me what you are feeling and how I can help you get back to normal."

Elizabeth gazed at her younger sister analyzing their differences. Alicia was slightly shorter than her sister was, with slightly lighter hair was, they each had blue eyes, the resemblance was there and they both were beautiful women. The younger one had always had more confidence. She felt their father had been partial to Alicia and that was why he spoiled her and had always been a sore point in the older sibling's life. These observances had caused depression to set in at times, but she had always been able to handle it until today. Now she found her spirit was in decline and she could not get in control of the beast that was causing it.

Elizabeth starred at her younger sister, then sat up reached for her pillow behind her and flung it at Alicia hitting her in the face.

"What was that for?"

"What do you mean what was that for? You just said you wanted me let it all out. Well, I am going to let it all out." She laughed as she grabbed another pillow hitting Alicia once again in the face.

"Ouch. That hurts. Stop that."

"Oh, it hurts you poor baby. I have watched you be coddled your whole life. Whatever Lisha wants she gets. You make me so mad I could swear."

"Lizzie, what's wrong with you?"

"What's wrong with me? Nothing, nothing is wrong now that father is gone and cannot protect you anymore. I can say anything I want to you. I can make you cry. I can laugh at you. I don't have to swallow your silly little back talk any longer." Elizabeth said reaching for an even larger pillow to throw at her

"No, you don't. You're not going to get by with that big sister.' With that, Alicia grabbed a sandwich and threw it at her this time hitting *her* in the face.

"Ok, if that's how you want it, that's how you get it missy."

The two sisters laughed and yelled as they ran around the room trying to miss the flying food, and picked up anything they could get their hands on to throw.

Beatrice and Miss Pendle opened the door to see what the commotion was only to receive a soaring sandwich in their face.

"Stop. Girls Stop. Look at this room. Look at your clothes. What is going on?"

Beatrice asked out of breath trying to miss the food missiles.

"Alicia wanted me to let it all out. So, I am. So, what's the problem now? I was just doing as I was told." Elizabeth cried out the words, and then sobbed uncontrollably.

The three women held her as she shook and cried until she was totally exhausted and there were no tears left.

Beatrice and Miss Pendle cleaned up the room while the two sparring sisters took a shower to cool off in Alicia's room.

"Do you feel better?" Alicia smiled.

"What do you think? Can't you tell I'm mad as hell at you for all the years I had to put up with you and father and the favorite daughter and she can do anything she wants routine year after year?"

"Lizzie, I didn't know. I didn't realize how deeply you must have felt about my relationship with father. I just would never let him upset me. I stood up to him and there were times I'd wished you had. I didn't realize how unfair father was to you. You just woke me up to fact that you thought I was a spoiled brat."

"You didn't know that until tonight?"

"I *didn't* know until tonight. It seems so simple, doesn't it? But I honestly didn't know. I must have been so self-involved it clouded the treatment you were receiving from father. I can see it now. How can I ever make it up to you?"

"You can't. This is something I need to get a handle on. I need to get some help. Know any good doctors, maybe a good shrink?"

"No, but we can find one. I think it is a great idea and I will come with you if you want so we can get this out for the last time. I don't want any more pillow or food rockets in the face."

"Sorry, but you asked for it remember?" She smiled not wanting to allow the stress she had just released return.

"I did my big sweet sister." She said running to her and giving her a big hug, which made them cry. Then laughing and again crying, as they talked the rest of the night 'getting it all out in the open once and for all to help end Elizabeth's years of festering negative feelings towards Alicia.'

# Chapter Four

"Alicia Rose just phoned. She invited me, all of us friends from university with Elizabeth to come to Roselyn for a surprise luncheon. I guess Lizzie is having trouble overcoming her father's death. I said I would come and would phone the rest of our little group and invite them. She didn't know where everyone was now except for me. Her attorney found me from my divorce papers. I am not comfortable with him handing out my information like that, I'm going to phone him and let him know about it. Oh, well guess it is for a good cause." Beth told Zoë.

"I'm sure he knew what he was doing. They all stick together you know. If it were a matter of allowing just anyone having your personal information that would definitely be a different matter."

"You know, there are times you really are brilliant."

"And you know there are times when you really are sarcastic."

The two friends laughed at each other and accepted their lot in life. One sarcastic and one almost brilliant. Zoë knew Beth and her other friends thought she was an air head but she didn't care anymore. At first it hurt her feelings when they'd laugh at her and had to take extra care to explain different situations to her that she didn't understand. They'd laugh and say, 'here we go again, Zoë needs an explanation …' As time went by though she could see some of the ones that had made fun of her ended up not enjoying life today as much as she was. She thought, she who laughs last, does laugh the best and the longest'.

"Are you going to the luncheon? I really miss her, we were close for a while until, well her father interfered." Beth said.

"I suppose I should. I always liked Elizabeth but she was in her own little world. She wasn't really with it was she?"

"What do you mean, not with it? I thought she was just shy. I liked her straightforwardness. She could get carried away at times though with her twisting words around. Remember how frustrated we'd get?"

"That is so true. Sometimes I'd get headaches and have to go home.  I Hope we can catch up on all the news about everyone we knew. Maybe at the luncheon we'll be able to do that. I think it could be very interesting."

"My, my, Scarlet, I do declare you are becoming a very perceptive little woman."

"Aren't we the little southern belle, I forgot about your little routine. It is all coming back. I hope it will be a good thing."

They laughed and reminisced looking forward to the reunion of their friends from younger days.

Alicia, Beatrice and Miss Pendle were trying nonchalantly to get Elizabeth to wear something nice for the surprise luncheon without her knowing why. It hadn't been easy to maneuver her into something dressy for that time of day. She had gotten into the habit of sweats and jeans were her main wardrobe since her father was not around to see how she looked. She had gotten 'slothful' as she used to use that term for Alicia and how she dressed at home. Now that statement fitted her. She definitely had changed.

"Miss Elizabeth, lunch is ready, Mrs. Waverly said you and Alicia can come to the dining room and enjoy a nice afternoon. She went all out for you." Beatrice winked at Alicia.

"Ok, I'm ready and hungry. Let's go little sis"

When Bea opened the large double doors to the formal dining room and when Elizabeth saw her friends sitting there, her mouth flew open and then yelled. "Where did you all come from? Why are you here?"

"Well, most of us came from London and some from other parts of the U.K. and even one of us from Paris. As for *why* we are here, isn't it obvious we are here for you my little 'red rose'." Beth announced with the nick name she had for Elizabeth.

"How nice to see you all. I am so overwhelmed. So that's why the dress this time of day. Alicia and Beatrice made me put this dress on or otherwise I'd be quite casual."

The friends chatted and laughed the afternoon away. They updated their lives while they had been apart. The good the bad and the not so good parts of their lives they willingly shared with each other. They were happy to have this chance to relive their happy days in their younger days and were very forthcoming with events in their lives. The reunion was a success.

The guest of honor could feel the burdens that her father had placed upon her were lighter that day. It would take some time for her to completely recover from her isolated and lonely past.

"It is so good to see you, Elizabeth, how are you doing?" Asked Beth

"I am doing very well, thank you. How are you and what have you been doing?"

"I was married as you know. Sorry you couldn't come to the wedding. I have twin sons.

"Two children?"

"Elizabeth, I was married for seven years. But now I'm divorced."

"Seven years? That long? I have so much to catch up on, don't I? With all of you? I am so glad we can spend this time together today and I hope we can do this often. Zoë, how have you been? Are you married?"

"I am doing well, I have never been married but I have a job at the BBC in the advertisement and design department, I love working there. It gives me a secure feeling to be part of it. "

"Are you going to teach art history? I remember after graduation how excited you were to be able to teach." Zoë asked.

"You should do that. What better time than now? You are at loose ends so do it." Beth insisted.

"Maybe I will, I will think about it."

The room was alive with chatter about their lives. Their good news and some bad news let Elizabeth know what she had missed in the past at that start of her new life with her neglected friends which had been no fault of her own.

The room overflowed with laughter trying t help their friend by brightening her very shallow, dull and drab life. Some of the things she found they had lives filled with  the most mundane things, yet she hadn't had a life of any kind other than taking care of her father.

"What about men? Are you ready for some male companionship? We can fix you up with some that we know. "Beth asked.

"No, I'm not quite ready for that.?

"Oh, come now. You can't tell me you're not ready for some big gorgeous hunk that you could have fun with."

"Not yet. Maybe later. I'll let you know."

"What about Anthony? Have you seen him lately?"

Elizabeth was stunned at the question. He had been a close friend she went with when she was at Cambridge. Then later after his graduation for a while until he left for further art studies in Europe, especially Italy and France.

"I don't know where he is, I haven't seen him in several years."

"I heard he was in Paris. He was doing very well with his paintings. I guess he is still there."

Elizabeth sighed. Glad that was over. She didn't want to have that worry placed on her so soon; she was not ready for Mr. Anthony Chadwick in her newly liberated though uncertain new life.

"Why don't you take a cruise? Take a Mediterranean Cruise? You could find someone aboard ship maybe? A shipboard romance like the movies?"

"I'll think about it." Elizabeth said curtly wanting to stop the topic of men.

She could never be comfortable around them. She tried to overcome her feelings that all men were like her father, domineering and hard to live with, all she wanted to do when she was with them was to twist their words around and make them eat everyone they'd said, especially the ones she felt were insincere, so men were nowhere to found on her 'to do' list.

The gathering had been a success. She was glad it was so enjoyable and that nothing drastic had been planned for her by them. She could tell though it wouldn't be long before they would be planning something. Yes, she thought. 'They will be up to something, especially Beth and Zoë.

35

As she took a stroll in the garden to see how her roses were growing, she couldn't shake the memories of Anthony. Remembering how much she did like the tall blondish young man from university and how attentive he had been until he had met Mr. Rose. She could tell it didn't take him long to find out the protective father was not thrilled about his daughter having a relationship with this person from Cornwall and only wanted to be an artist. 'What kind of man is that who only wants to be an artist? 'He asked Elizabeth sarcastically.

The thoughts of those days with Anthony did warm her heart as she recalled time spent with him. She remembered how he talked about living on the 'Continent' and going to all the museums that housed the incredible art he read about from books he was reading in his art classes and wanted to copy some of the old masters. She thought how talented he was and why he wanted to copy someone else's work when he could produce his own beautiful original art.

She contemplated her art classes; she wanted to teach art history and what if she did apply for a job?

'I wonder where he is....?' She thought as she pinched off some extra buds growing too thick on her rose bushes.

Gardening had been a lifesaver for her. It gave her a release for her stressful and controlled life. Her favorite flowers of course were roses. Not only rose bushes but all types. Long stemmed roses were first on her list.

'Yes, I wonder where he is and what he is doing. Oh, I'm sure he is married and has children by now. What am I thinking? Don't be so presumptuous. I can't allow myself to ever think about him again. I am not ready for male companionship anyway. I have to take it one step at a time.

# *Chapter Five*

Alicia nervously slipped into her wedding gown making a sigh of relief when she found it fit perfectly.

Elizabeth carefully zipped the back of the soft white silk dress. The time and alterations were worth the effort. The bride to be was radiant. Her long medium brown hair piled high on her head had been secured with an abundant supply of hair pins. She'd joked about not being able to go through the security check at the airport with all the metal in her hair as the bell would go off if she did. The veil that was attached to the small subtle silk white rose crown added to the dress with the enormously long train that the grooms young nephews would carry.

Every detail was perfect. The only thing sad about that day would be the looming fact Mr. Rose would not be there to walk his beautiful daughter down the long isle in the ancient Cathedral in London.

"There, you are. All ready for the groom. You are the most beautiful bride I have ever seen in my life." Elizabeth cried. She had to dab her tears softly not wanting to disturb her carefully applied make up.

"Thank you for everything Lizzie. I love you. I want you to get married someday. I want you to fall in love with a gorgeous hunk like Jordan and live happily ever after. Don't wait too long, find someone now. Ok? Promise me you will?"

"I will, I promise." She said handing Alicia her bouquet of small pink roses.

They carefully went downstairs and got into the limousine that Travis had shinning beyond belief. He'd spent the whole day before preparing it for this special occasion. His farewell gift to Miss Alicia Rose.

Jordan Lindquist was an attorney. He was from an aristocratic family which Mr. Rose accepted into the family straight away, but wanted them to wait until he died to get married. He wanted them to be sure they could have a happy life together and didn't want them to 'rush into anything'. The truth of the matter was he was selfish and controlling and didn't want to share his youngest daughter with anyone.

The couple did as he said and now, they were free to live the life they'd looked forward to for such a long time.

They would be living in his father and mother's estate not far from Roselyn. Alicia was happy with the decision to live there. The estate was large enough to never know who was there and who was not, they would have plenty of privacy and also when the older couple passed away, they would inherit it. The newlyweds would be having children right away and fill the place with noise and laughter as they had talked about endlessly.

Elizabeth stood watching her little sister slowly walk in step with Jordan's father down the aisle. Dressed in a long pale rose color silk dress, with her sun-streaked hair piled high upon her head for the occasion she was happy for her sister who had waited so long for this occasion.

All the brides' maids were dressed alike in the same long rose silk gown and the groom's men were in black ties and tails as was the groom. They were all picture perfect. The Rose father would have been proud of both of his daughters that eventful day.

The reception at the Savoy Hotel in London was extraordinary. It had just been renovated and it was outstanding.

Everyone was excited to celebrate with the newly wedded couple in the landmark hotel.

"Did you see Anthony?" Beth asked Elizabeth.

"Anthony? Anthony Chadwick?

"Yes, he's here, didn't you see him?"

"No, how did he know about the wedding?"

"I don't know; ask Alicia, she sent the invitations."

"There, over by the bar, see him?"

"Yes, I do now." She said softly.

"He's coming over. Ooh, he looks great. Life has been good to Mr. Chadwick."

Zoë whispered to Elizabeth.

Anthony Chadwick was an artist of considerable talent. His love of the masters was evident from the paintings he had given her. The one she liked the most was though the one he'd painted of her in her blue ball gown that still hung in the library. Creighton Rose had no idea Anthony painted it or it would have been thrown out as he didn't want his daughter to have anything to do with the artist from Cornwall.

The tall blonde attractive man smiled as he walked toward the three whispering friends. Elizabeth's boyfriend from school that had faded from her life. All her wonderful thoughts and emotional sensations washed over her.

"Hello ladies. How have you been?" He asked grinning at them feeling their surprise with his attendance at the wedding.

"Fine, we've been just fine, how have you been?" Zoë stammered.

"Hello, Miss Rose, how are you?"

"Fine too, I'm fine too. How did you know about the wedding?" She said her heart started to pound.

"I received the invitation in the mail like everyone else."

"I see you haven't changed your sarcastic nature since our university days.

"No, I haven't, have you?" He kept up the banter with Elizabeth as Beth and Zoë slipped away leaving them alone to get reacquainted.

"No, I guess not. Where do you live now? I heard you moved to Paris, is that true?"

"Yes, it is, I live there now. I go back and forth between Italy and Paris. I do a lot of work in both places.

"You must be very accomplished to be able to sell paintings in those shops. Only the best artists are featured there. I am very happy for you Anthony. I know that was your dream."

"Thank you for remembering. I didn't know if you would even remember me after all these years."

"We were good friends, how could I forget my friend?"

"Is that what we were Elizabeth, just friends?"

"What do you mean? Just friends?"

"Please, let's sit down at that table and reminisce the good ole days."

"Are you married?" He asked her.

"No, you?"

"No. Not now, that is."

"What do you mean, not now?"

"I was married for a couple of years, but it didn't work out. She wanted something I couldn't give her."

"Oh, what was that?"

"My heart." He said flatly, as he stared into her sparkling blue eyes for her reaction.

"I'm sorry about that, didn't you love her when you got married?"

"I thought I did. But I soon found out I didn't."

"That's sad. I am sorry. It must have been a painful time in your life. How are your parents? Are they still in Cornwall?"

"It wasn't too bad, I got over it. Yes, my parents are doing fine and they still live in Cornwall. I have to go there tomorrow, why don't you ride along? I'm sure they would love to see you."

"I don't know." Elizabeth said starring down at the empty plate on the expertly set table.

"I heard about your father. Sorry. I am sure you miss him. He was your life, wasn't he?"

"Yes, yes he was. I do miss him, but I am getting better now. It gets better each day and now I am reconnecting with my friends so my future is looking brighter."

"That's good, now how about going with me tomorrow?"

"Alright, I will. The salty air will be good for me. "

"That's what you need is more salt." He laughed.

"Yeah, so do you, my salty friend."

"Why do you keep calling me friend?"

"That's what you are."

"Oh, I am?" He laughed remembering how deep his feelings had been for her and now they were coming back to haunt him.

The pair enjoyed the memories from their past. They talked and danced until it was time for the bride and groom to go.

Alicia threw her bouquet at Elizabeth and caught it to her surprise.

"That has a meaning you know. You will be the next bride." Anthony commented, wishing he could start where they left off so abruptly several years ago.

"Do you believe in old wives tales?"

"Sure, I do, I believe in that one."

They sat back down at the table and continued the renewal of their friendship until it was time to go.

Anthony escorted her to the limousine and Travis that had been waiting for her.

"See you tomorrow. I'll pick you up at ten o'clock. Will you ask Mrs. Waverly if she would make us some of her sandwiches hope she remembers the ones I liked the meaty ones? I'm glad she's doing well. Tell her I miss her cooking."

"Sure, I know her and she will be happy to make us a picnic lunch. She will be happy to see you. So be sure to come in and say hello."

"Sounds good. See you at ten." He said as he gave her a kiss on the cheek.

Elizabeth got ready for bed. As she changed into her pajamas and looked at her reflection in the bathroom mirror and thought, 'Not bad for almost forty.' She thought to herself climbing into bed.

"Miss Elizabeth, Anthony Chadwick is here are you ready to come down stairs?"

"In a minute, have him wait for me in the library, that's his favorite place. Also tell Mrs. Waverly he's here and wants to see her."

"Yes, miss, I will."

"Mr. Anthony Chadwick. Where have you been? I've missed you."

"Well, I've been here and there and now I'm here. I didn't know if you would remember me."

"No, I didn't forget you and I can tell you haven't changed a bit you big 'Jesse'."

"Ah, music to my ears, Mrs. Waverly and her velvet toned voice and the extraordinary way she makes me feel right at home." He laughed enjoying the fact she even remembered him.

"What's going on in here? "

"Mr. Chadwick…"

"Please just call me Anthony."

"Alright, then, Anthony and I are catching up on things. The basket is on the table by the door; pick it up on the way out. I filled it with Mr……I mean Anthony's favorite sandwiches and I even remembered his favorite cookies and cakes and there's a large flask of tea." She said happily at the thought this young man was in their lives again.

"You spoil us; I always had the best memories of this house mostly they were because of you."

"Now, you must have kissed the 'Blarney Stone' on your way here." She said pleased at his remarks.

Anthony walked over and kissed her on the cheek and thanked her and told her good bye as she walked out the door of the mammoth library.

"This is *the* most incredible room I have ever been in. Sorry for sounding like a peasant but I am serious. You have books here that the libraries don't even have."

"You don't sound like a peasant. You never have. Why would you say such a thing?"

"I don't exactly fit into your world do I Miss Rose?"

"Why do you say that?"

"Don't you remember your father and how he would look me up and down and then scowl each time I said hello?"

"Yes, but that was just because he didn't want me to have any male friends. It wasn't just you."

"I beg your pardon. Later on, I found out when Alicia started going with Jordan your father was ok with him."

"Well, he didn't want them to get married until after he died though. So, I wouldn't feel too bad. My father was not an easy man."

All Anthony could do to respond to that profound comment about her father was to raise his eyebrows, look upward and say an 'amen' silently.

"Let's go, we have a long trip, remember we have to spend the night. I forgot to remind you."

"I remembered. Suitcase in hand and I'm ready to go."

"You sound chipper this morning."

"Chipper? I don't know about that, but I feel good and I am looking forward to this trip to Cornwall. I haven't been there since…well since you know."

"I don't know. Refresh my memory."

"When we had our discussion about …my father."

"Oh, I forgot about that." Anthony lied. He didn't want to remember. It had been too painful.

"Let's be off mademoiselle, your carriage awaits you."

"Is this your car or are you hiring it?"

"It's just a rental. My cars are at home. I don't bring them with me." He laughed as he drove through the gate and into the traffic.

"We are going to start out by being sarcastic? You just be prepared. I'm fully able to hold my own now. So, all I have to say is bring it on."

"Fully able to hold your own? Have you forgotten our rounds of word wars? You were the most…" He didn't finish what he was going to say and quickly changed the subject. "When are you going to learn how to drive?"

"How do you know I can't drive? Maybe I drive every day."

"You just can't have a normal conversation, can you? You never answer my questions. You never have conversed in a straight line. You zigzag all over the place. Do you know we never, not one time had a decent conversation? A conversation that was either meaningful, or fruitful."

"What do you mean 'fruitful'?"

"You know, discussing anything and actually resolving any issue and coming to any sort of conclusion. We always left things muddled and in the air. Sometimes we would actually confuse things even more after we'd discussed it rather than when we first began."

"You sound confused now. I don't understand what you are trying to say."

"Skip it. "He took a deep breath trying to calm down." Let's pretend we just met and are finding about each other for the first time. We can play a 'game of I don't know you and you don't know me. 'How does that sound?"

"Stupid. Just stupid. Why are you acting so strange?"

"What do you mean strange? I'm just desperately trying to make a point."

"Ok, what point is that?"

"You know, oh forget it. I'm taking you back home. I can't take this all the way to Cornwall."

"What?"

"You heard me. I am turning around and taking you back to 'Roselyn'. Period end."

"Fine with me, I wasn't looking forward to that long trip anyway." Elizabeth tried to mask her disappointment.

They sat silence on the way back to Roselyn. Anthony couldn't take anymore of the nonsensical conversation with her. They always did that and now he was not going to even go there for a day. No more he promised himself. No more pain and uncertainty from her. No more.

Elizabeth had him insert her card for entry through the secured gate and waited for the large gate to open.

"Here we are. See you around. I'll get your luggage."

"Never mind. I have it. Good bye." Elizabeth stomped off towards the massive wooden double door that Hodges had just opened for her with a total surprised look on his face after only saying goodbye less than an hour ago.

Elizabeth ran up to her room and flung herself on her bed sobbing out of control. She was so hurt and embarrassed from her treatment from Anthony that she vowed she would never, never talk to him again and there would never be a man in her life. That was a promise she made that day to reassure her tender feelings it would never happen again and that was final, 'period end' as Anthony had just remarked.

# *Chapter Six*

The radiant sky painted the Pacific Ocean a neon orange announcing to the western coast of California, that this day was over and the night was almost nigh.

Timothy Rose found it comforting with the close of that very profitable day. He was satisfied with the days' work and he felt confidant for his future and had taken years of struggle and constant work.

He was happy now, that he'd made the decision to move his 'Rose Import, Export Company' to Los Angeles from London, twenty years earlier. It hadn't been easy for him. His business in London was established and there was almost no effort in maintaining a very comfortable life. Even by London standards.

When his wife passed away, he felt the emptiness of her absence and made every effort to secure close relationships with his children, David now, twenty-four, and Karri, twenty-two. They were close and always felt free to voice their opinions.

He found his growing resentment with Creighton and the ongoing sibling rivalry and was more than a normal discord and grew even worse when his older brother had not been able to have a son but only two daughters. The relentless snide remarks about David telling everyone 'he looked like he wasn't all there', was incredibly insensitive and unbearable. The tension and hatred grew so extreme that Timothy's only recourse was to move as far away from London as possible. With his wife no longer there to help heal his wounds from the anguish inflicted by Creighton, he decided it was time for him to move his children and company to America.

Timothy was glad to hear his brother had finally died. It was a relief to know even though they didn't live close in proximity there had been the invisible thread of the cutting words that haunted him, and now he might be able to heal from all the years of torture that echoed through their years together.

Going outside, he decided to have his meal there and enjoy the splendor of the setting sun that showered the deck surrounding the large ranch style house that was located on the beach.

Yes, he was pleased with the way things had turned out and thoroughly loved being with David and Karri.

"Dad, I'm home." David called out to his father.

"I'm out here."

"You're home early. Do you have plans tonight?"

"No, I just wanted to have dinner with you and maybe beat you a game of cheese."

"Ha. You and who did you bring to help you accomplish that great feat?"

"Just me. I beat you last time, remember?"

"Yes, I guess you did, I forgot, I guess you did."

"Yeah, your memory is very convenient."

"Is Karri here?"

"Not, yet, I don't know her plans tonight."

"Mr. Rose are you ready for dinner now?" Mrs. Sullivan asked. She'd been his housekeeper and cook for several years after he'd been able to hire her.

"Yes, David and I are. I don't know about Karri though."

"She phoned and said she will be here shortly."

"Good. We'll finally have a family dinner."

"Karri, we were just talking about you. Glad you're here. Let's eat."

"I'm starved." David said sitting down.

David was tall and handsome like his father, with slightly darker hair and the same hazel green eyes but he didn't have the exquisite British accent that announced to everyone he was not an American.

Karri was tall and graceful even though she was considered a 'tom boy'. Her hair was light brown also had her father's color eyes. She was very attractive.

"Dad, I wanted to ask you a question without you blowing up. Ok? Why didn't we go to Aunt Alicia's wedding?" Karri asked.

"Why? You know very well why. Don't start the Rose family routine. We are the Rose family here in L.A. that's all."

"Why are you so bitter?"

"I'll tell you why. Creighton William Rose is why."

"But Dad, he's dead now, can't we go see our Aunt Alicia and Aunt Elizabeth?"

"No. Absolutely not."

"They always send the nicest cards and gifts for Christmas and our birthdays, even you get them. Why can't we just visit? Just David and I, you don't have to go. Please, I want to see them. I want to see where you grew up. David and I both want to go visit them. "

"Since when have you two been interested in taking a trip to London?"

"Well, since we heard Uncle Creighton passed away."

"Dad it would just be for a vacation. You need to get away from business for a while and this could be a meaningful trip if you would only listen to us. We have discussed this quite a bit lately."

Timothy reflected on their words and absorbed what they were saying and could not come up with a reason not to go to London and visit Roselyn.

"Let me think about it for awhile. I guess since he's gone there would be no problem with just a short stay. I wouldn't mind seeing Elizabeth and Alicia again. They were nice girls. They evidently got that from their mother. Let me get some business taken care of and I'll let you know. You don't have anything going this summer before school starts again in August?"

"Free as birds." David replied excitedly.

"Dad. That is great. I love you." Karri said hugging her father.

The plane landed smoothly at Heathrow Airport. The American Rose family deplaned with the other passengers rumpled from the long flight and they still had to go through customs.

"Dad. Look. Over there. Do you see the man in the uniform holding that sign? 'Timothy Rose and family, I will take you to Roselyn.' That must be their chauffeur. Wow. This is great. We are going in style. "David almost yelled.

"Calm down David. Act like this is normal. I don't want you getting too loud and please show some manners, both of you, ok?"

"Yes, father, anything you say father." Karri said mockingly.

"Here we are what your name is?"

"Travis, sir. Are you Mr. Timothy Rose?"

"Yes, I am and these are my children, David and Karri."

"I will pick up your luggage when you are through customs. Just wave at me and I will be over to get them for you sir."

"Thank you, Travis. It shouldn't take long, doesn't look like the line is too long."

The London traffic was heavy as usual. The limousine slowly wound around the round-a-bouts as Travis maneuvered it over to the proper exit.

David and Karri sat mesmerized at the amount of traffic and the unusual feeling of driving on the wrong side of the road even though they weren't actually driving, but were only passengers.

The heavy gas and oil mixture smell was quite new to them. They noticed London definitely had the aroma of a very old and heavily concentrated driving population. The nearly eight million citizens that lived there all seemed to be in their automobiles that day.

Finally, they saw the gate that held the brass plate with the 'Roselyn' crest on it as Travis carefully stopped, swiped the security card and waited for the gate to open.

"This is incredible." Karri whispered to David.

"I know."

"Now remember what I told you. Please use your manners. Don't act like delinquents."

"Dad. I resent that. We have never acted like delinquents. Why should we start now?" David protested his father's sudden panic about their behavior.

"I know, I'm sorry, but this place brings out the worst in me. It is an instant reaction for me to be critical when I'm here. Sorry. I will try to relax. Now that the critic is gone maybe I can enjoy this visit."

"Good, I hope so. Now you must learn to behave." Karri teased her dad in return for him being so cautious with them that they might embarrass him.

Timothy Rose was taller than his older brother. He was also more handsome. He had more going for him than he ever knew when he was younger and still living under the scrutiny of Creighton, even before they had children to worry about the Rose trust. He could never understand why Creighton despised him.

"Timothy. This must be David. Karri. I am so glad to see you. What a long time it's been. You children were only toddlers when you moved to America.

Your rooms are ready. Timothy you will stay in your old room and Karri and David are on either side of you. Travis will help you with your luggage. You can get unpacked and take a shower. We will have dinner at eight o'clock. I will let you alone until then. If you need anything please let me know. Timothy, you know how to ring for service?"

"Yes, if it's still the same system."

"Yes, it is. So, I will see you later."

"Dad, I am overwhelmed. Just think you *lived* here as a child and left when you were how old?"

"I lived here off and on during my university years. Then left for good when your mother and I got married that was a year before you were born. So, twenty-five years. It's been a long time since I've been back. Nothing has changed. Everything looks the same." He said looking around

"This is it. My room, so pick which room you want Karri and David you can have the other one. She said either side of me. So go for it."

The tender feelings of the past arose in Timothy stronger than he'd ever imagined. Remembering his mother and father whom he loved very much had been clouded by the hatred he had for Creighton. He'd forgotten the good times. The memories of the chess games with his father after dinner, the walks through the luxuriant gardens with his mother washed warmly over him. He did have a good childhood. He'd forgotten. He had allowed his negative powerful feelings for his older brother block the good part of his life at 'Roselyn'.

"Timothy, tell me all about your lives in California. I've always wanted to visit Disneyland, and all the tourist attractions. Is it as beautiful as they say it is?" Elizabeth asked as they were being served dinner.

"Yes, it is. We would love for you to visit us. Let us know when and we would want you to stay with us. We have a home on the beach. You would love it. Please anytime."

"Thank you, I'll think about it, I'm not quite sure when I could get away."

"Just know the invitation is always open." Timothy said.

"David, what courses are you taking?"

"I am actually going to be an attorney; I'm going to Stanford. It's a good program and not that far and I go home on the weekends."

"When will you graduate?"

"I have another year before I can take the bar exam. I will be glad when it's over. I'm ready to just work and live a regular life."

"Do you have a girlfriend?"

"No, just a friend, nothing serious."

"That's not true. He does have someone serious. Her name is Sarah and she is also going to law school. "

"Karri. That's not totally true. Yes, we go together, but we are *not* serious."

"Alright you two., that's enough. Karri let David alone, don't intrude into his personal life."

"Ok, sorry, I just thought....."

"Well, don't just think." David warned her.

"Karri, what are you taking in university?"

"Just the basics now and get them out of the way, maybe by then I'll know what I want to do."

"That's ok, I didn't know what I wanted when I first started. It will come."

"What did you major in?"

"I ended up getting my 'Art History' credentials and I am presently thinking about applying for a job."

"Good for you. I am sure you will enjoy it. Where did you go?"

"Cambridge, like your father."

"That must be some place." Karri said softening her exuberance.

"I'd like to see the campus when you get the chance. I've heard so much about it from Dad." David added trying not to sound too eager.

"We can do that, whenever you want to do, just let me know so Travis can take us."

"No, please, we are going to rent cars while we're here. Well, I am driving at first then I'll help David and Karri get acclimatized to the left side of the road." Timothy smiled.

"Yeah, he thinks we're not capable."

"I didn't mean that Karri, all I said was for safety's sake we need to let you get acquainted with the way they drive here." Timothy interrupted.

"I don't care just so we can drive. I want to see everything here in this beautiful country, the United Kingdom, the land of my birth. "David said with the astonished proclamation of the return to his homeland.

# Chapter Seven

David jumped out of bed quickly showered and ran down stairs for breakfast finding his father and sister already seated in the formal dining room with the large chandelier hanging over the large wooden antique table that had served meals for generations of Roses.

"You are early; I thought I would be the first one down. What are the plans for today?"

"Nothing except to get you both driving. I don't want to hear any more about how mean I am not letting you drive. We'll get Travis to take us to the car rental after we finish breakfast. Did you meet Mrs. Waverly?"

"Who is Mrs. Waverly?"

"She's the cook. She has been since I was in university. She has a large staff now to help her; she does the cooking through them. You will like her."

"Just like the old BBC series, 'Upstairs, Downstairs.' "? David asked.

"Yes, just like that." Timothy remembered.

"I can't even imagine what it was like to live here as a child. Did you have toys and games? I'd like to see pictures of you when you were growing up, does Elizabeth have albums we could see?" Karri asked.

"I would think she still has them, mum kept them in the library. We'll ask her to let us see them tonight. But first I want to get you in cars."

"Mum? That's the first time I've heard you talk about your mother. I didn't know you called her 'mum'."

"I am British, or have you forgotten? That was the name for our mother, 'mum', what's so funny about that?"

"It just sounds odd for you to talk like that. I'm not used to this new Dad we're discovering. It's neat." Kari laughed.

"I don't know what's so new about this; I thought I talked about my life here quite a bit when you were growing up."

"No, you didn't. I don't remember anything except Creighton despised you."

"Really? I'm sorry I didn't share the good memories I had growing up here. I'll have to tell you all about it while we're here. We'll have Elizabeth get the albums out and I'll check to see where our toys and games are. I am sure they must be here. Nothing is ever thrown away. Everything is saved for the future generations."

"Wonderful. I can't wait to see how you were when you were young. Well, not that you're old now." Karri exclaimed.

The day was eventful. Timothy patiently droves around London to prove it was not as easy as it looked to drive with the driver's seat on the right side of the car and the heavy traffic and on the left side of the street. Then there was the inevitable round-a-bouts. He allowed them to each take turns until he thought they could manage without him. They had to drive together though, no solo driving for now.

The trio drove back to the estate and was told dinner would be at eight o'clock in the formal dining room, which meant formal dress.

"Dad. This is archaic. Who dresses in a tux just for dinner?" David asked.

"We do while we are here. You wanted to see Roselyn and experience my life, well here it is, formal dress and all. Get going and I want to see you both all 'spit and shinned'." Timothy laughed and grateful he made them bring their formal attire.

The massive table was glistening from the chandelier and candles illuminating the crystal glassware with golden trim. The soft pink and white flower arrangements from the garden and proved how productive Roselyn had been made.

Miss Pendle had seen to it that everything was as perfect as Elizabeth had ordered.

Mrs. Waverly also had seen to it that the dinner would be Timothy's favorite, Roast beef, Yorkshire pudding, roasted potatoes and gravy, then for dessert he would always want her chocolate mud cake and ice cream. Never salad, he told her 'Salads were for rabbits.'

David and Karri stopped at the doorway trying to absorb the grandiose scene in front of them.

Hodges helped them to their chairs that were arranged around the end of the table to be able to converse with one another.

"Hello, I hope you had a good day." Elizabeth greeted them.

"We did, we drove and got acquainted with London." David replied.

"That is wonderful. Now you can teach me how to drive. That is on my list of things I want to do."

"I don't know about David and Karri teaching you, but I will be glad to, you just tell me when." Timothy said.

"How about tomorrow? Are you busy?"

"No, I have no agenda while I'm here, I'm just along for the ride with David and Karri."

"Alright, tomorrow it is."

"Elizabeth, we wanted to see the albums of Dad when he was growing up. Could we have a look at them tonight?"

"Yes, certainly, we will get copies made for you if you'd like. We can take them to the photographers tomorrow. That would work out well. Timothy you could drive there and we could drop them off before I start me lesson?"

"Sounds good to me. I would like to have them for the future."

David and Karri forgot about their protested formal clothing and enjoyed the evening meal that had been so carefully planned for them.

Elizabeth led them to the enormous library where the albums were kept.

"You may look around if you want while I find the volumes we want to look at. It may take a few minutes.

Make yourselves at home. Uncle Timothy this is your home too. You know I have always felt uncomfortable about the trust and Roselyn and in the end was given to me even though I was not a male heir. I hope you understand how I have wrestled with this for years and I still am today."

He smiled at her knowing what she meant. That now it was her estate. The estate that had been his home many years ago and now today would have been thrilled for it to be handed down to his son David, but knew for sure that would never happen.

"Here they are, we can sit at the desk and look at them."

"This one is dated May 1961. You were a year old?" Karri asked.

"Yes, that is me. I'd forgotten how beautiful mum was. She's been dead for so long… father was handsome too. It's funny how forgetful we get as we grow older letting our memories of parent's features grow dim. I always thought what a striking couple they were. I haven't thought about them in so long. It's a shame David and Karri won't know them."

"I know, I vaguely remember them. Father didn't talk about them. I don't ever remember him talking about them, isn't that strange, now that I think about it."

"Dad, you were so cute. Look at your school uniform."

"Oh, yes, the old school uniforms. I thought we looked silly, but that was part of life. We tried to ignore them and focus on sports. Then we could change into something we felt comfortable in."

"Dad, here a journal I think you should read, this entry. "

"Whose is it?"

"It's Uncle Creighton's. It's dated August 20th, 1966.

"Today was one of those days I wanted to run and hide. I overheard father talking to his friend, Lionel, about the differences in his two sons. That the older one was awkward and he thought the younger one would be a very good athlete. He was always hoping the oldest one would take after him and enjoy polo and cricket but that he never could get him interested in sports. All he wanted to do was read books and go with as many girls as he could. He didn't have much hope the oldest son would be much more than a bookworm and womanizer.

My father never sees what books I am reading. I am going to be the best barrister that ever was and then I want to be in Parliament and argue with the Labor Party how off track they are.'

I am going to show him and mum. They both think their little Timothy is such a marvelous boy. I'll show them.'

"Dad. This is sad. Did you know he was treated this way by your parents? No wonder he hated you. Then to make matters worse you had the son he should have had." David said after reading the life of a very lonely and sad young man and what had been revealed in the obscure journals of his bitter uncle and now had a clearer picture of why he had treated his younger brother so badly.

"Let me see that." Timothy grabbed the book from him. "Has this been here all along? In this cabinet?"

"I guess so; I hardly ever come in here. Father was usually the only one that was in here." Elizabeth said as she suddenly found herself in a new world of her father's cry for attention and love from his parents.

"Did you know he felt this way about me when we were growing up?

"I had no idea. All I could understand about his resentment of you was that you had the son he wanted."

"Let's see, he must have been twenty-one. That's how old he was when he and mum were married. He was at university." Elizabeth exclaimed. "I was born the next year."

"Dad. It sounds like he never was able to please your mother and father. No wonder he hated you. I can see why. You didn't know how they treated him?" David asked.

"No, I was away at boarding school and he was also but at a different one. We only saw father and mum some weekends and holidays. I didn't know.

I was only six, when that entry was made, how could father know I would be good at sports at that age?"

Timothy sat holding the newly discovered journal starring at the flickering fire connecting his brother's treatment by their father sounding so partial to him.    This knowledge brought new feelings about his deceased brother.

Sadness overwhelmed him as he continued to read the journal, and found other volumes that contained the same topic, Creighton's endurance of Timothy.

The older brother had been fifteen when he'd started to feel a difference in his treatment from his parents and found this younger brother would over shadow him in every way, looks, athletic abilities, and finally the ability to father a son was the crux of things he'd had to bear, and truly set the pattern of resentment escalated as time went by.

Timothy's new insight brought a deep penetrating and overwhelming sorrow that derived from the journals containing poignant feelings entered into these journals by his older brother so long ago.

Elizabeth sat starring into the glowing fire trying to reconcile her negative feelings for her father into positive ones attached to a new found love for him. Saddened by the fact she had to wait until after his death to find out about the revelations about his life and treatment of his mother and father and the partiality to Timothy, the younger brother. How she could identify with everything. There was still the perplexing question why he was partial to Alicia, what had she ever done to not be able to have his love and devotion.

Maybe she would find out. She was going to go through thoroughly all the journals to see if she could get an understanding. Maybe she was just waging a losing battle, but she must at least try.

# Chapter Eight

Elizabeth sat at her dressing table brushing her lustrous sun-streaked hair noticing for the first time in several years her true reflection and how attractive she was. The thoughts of anything cosmetic hadn't entered her mind for a long time and she hadn't noticed just how outdated she looked. 'I'm going to call Beth and Zoë to help me get a remodel.' She thought.

As she turned her head from side to side, she also became aware that her spacious bedroom suite was lacking the ambience to match the cheerful singing of the birds that morning outside the window partially covered with ivy. 'I think my bedroom is also going to get a makeover.' She laughed. 'This is going to be the start a new life…a new me…a new bedroom…. I wonder if Karri would like to join us. I'll ask her. We could get to know each other and we can show her more of London.'

"Beth, would you and Zoë be able to meet me for lunch? I have something I need your help with, how about one o'clock at "Paddy's?"

"Sure, I'll phone her and see if she can make it. What made you think of "Paddy's?"

"It just popped into my mind when I was talking to you. I just remembered it was one of our favorites. I haven't been there in eons."

"I haven't either. That sounds like fun. We'll, or at least I'll be there."

"Karri, are you there?" Elizabeth tapped on her door.

"Yes, come in, I just had my shower."

"Good, I was wondering if you would like to go with me today. Do you have any plans with your father and brother?"

"Not really, Dad was up late last night rereading Uncle Creighton's journals."

"I'm sad about that too. I had no idea my grandparents treated him so badly. My father never complained. He never said a word about them. That tells me I missed knowing my *real* father, the one that was enclosed in bitterness. I am so sorry for him, my feelings are very tender for him now and it is a good thing to remember him this way rather than the one he portrayed for all those years. I will talk to Alicia when she returns from her honeymoon. She will be happy to know our father wasn't as mean as we'd believed he was all those years."

"When will she be back? She's been on her honeymoon a long time."

"They should be back in a few weeks. They are still in Paris and will go on to the Mediterranean soon, and then they will return sometime next month."

"Where were you going?"

"Oh, yes, I forgot, I wanted to get a haircut and new make up so thought you might like to join me? I have a couple of friends we will meet for lunch first and then off to the spa. How does that sound?"

"Sure, I guess so. I'm not much into make-up, but I'll go.

You know, I didn't think you and I, because of our age difference, would be able to have a relationship, but maybe we can after all."

"I don't see why not, of course you are much younger, but we do have strong family connections. We need to always stay close. I want to take you to Cambridge one day too maybe David would like to go with us."

"I'm sure he will. He can't stop talking about that place.
"

Paddy's was a pub in north London where the three friends frequented while they were at university. It had the customary separated dining area London pubs were famous for. They weren't into alcohol when they'd seen how ignorant their friends would become when they were under the influence and some of them had serious car accidents as a result of it but the pub had provided a meeting place and they enjoyed the food as well.

"Elizabeth, over here." Zoë called out.

The atmosphere was the same since university days. The soft earthy colors of brown, tan, and red, and orange, with splashes of yellow table clothes hadn't changed.

Beth and Zoë were sitting at their favorite place next to the large black pained bay window.

"I'm so glad you could make it too Zoë. I want you both to meet my cousin, Karri. She is from Los Angeles, California. Isn't that wonderful?"

"Nice to meet you Karri, are you enjoying London?"

"It is very interesting, especially the driving. I feel awkward sitting on the left side as a passenger. I feel like I need to have the steering wheel in front of me.

I love the old buildings. It has been fascinating to know how old some of them are. We don't have anything like that at home. They tear down the old buildings and make malls out of them. I am beginning to see why people are protesting when they do this. We have no history compared to you. I never thought about the past very much until now. I want to see more."

"We will take you wherever you want to go. Just let me know." Elizabeth reassured her.

"Thank you, one place I want to see is 'Trafalgar Square'. I remember something about that name from history. I also want to see' Stone Hinge '"

"That is a plan. So, starting today we will see Trafalgar Square. It is just further downtown on our way to the spa."

"Spa?"

"That's what I wanted to talk to you about. I want to get my haircut and go to the spa and a makeover. I want to be refreshed. I am tired of looking tired. I want to start enjoying life again. It's been a long time since I've done anything luxurious."

"All right. I want to go with you. I need something too. It's been awhile since I've been there." Beth said.

"I should say so. Since her divorce, she hasn't budged from her house and children. I was wondering when she was going to get out of her doldrums."

Zoë confided.

"I'm sorry Beth; I didn't know you'd been depressed. I should have though. A divorce must be devastating."

"Yes, it is. Devastating is the word. When you find out one day your life was nothing but a lie it leaves you feeling totally rejected and worthless. Those feelings do not just go away. I have to work on it every day. Thank goodness, for my children or I wouldn't have a reason to even get up in the morning let alone go to therapy. I need to go to work. I just haven't had the energy to even look for a job.

"I am so sorry Beth. I had no idea. I was trying to survive my life with a demanding father that filled my days. I didn't have the thoughts or the time to get in touch with anyone, and there were times I didn't know what day it was. I look back now and wonder how I ever got through the fog. I was lost. Somewhere along the way I evolved into a robot with no thoughts or feelings other than what my father was thinking and feeling. "

"Now maybe we can pull ourselves together. Start a new beginning and pick up where we left off after university. The spa will be a good place to begin."

"All right, now we have those two settled how about you Karri?"

Zoë asked.

"Me? What do you mean?"

"Well, are you going to a university? What are you taking, and do you have a boyfriend?"

"Zoë, you're getting a little too personal, aren't you?"

"I don't see why. I was just interested in her life as a pretty young American girl that is the niece of Creighton Rose. Do you realize the prominence his name has here? "

"First of all, I do go to Stanford University in California. I don't know what I want to do yet so I am just taking the basic classes that I need to get out of the way and hopefully by then I'll know what I want to do for a career. No, I don't have a steady boyfriend. I had one but we broke up, I guess we outgrew each other after our high school days. We are still friends though and no, I didn't know that Uncle Creighton was a prominent man. Why was he prominent?"

"He was a barrister, then was an MP, which means he was a Minister in Parliament. "

"Elizabeth, that's what he was talking about in his journal. Remember?"

"What journal?"

"We found father's journals in the library last night and they revealed my grandparents were very partial to Uncle Timothy and that he could never measure up including having a male heir which was his self-imposed bitterness.

I was just an infant when they died in the boating accident. I never knew them and he didn't say anything about how they had treated him. He only kept his feelings in his journals."

"That is incredible. Now you can see why he was so bitter? That sure paints a different picture of him now. I can understand why now. Did Timothy know about this partiality?" Beth asked.

"No, he didn't. He is going through a hard time today…Beth, oh, well, we should get going. Are we ready to get beautiful?"

"I can't I have to get back to work. I'll go another time. Call me for evenings and weekends. I'm usually working the rest of the time. I do want to catch up on everything. Even Anthony."

"Who's he?" Karri asked.

"He's just someone I used to know. He lives in Paris now. I won't see him anymore."

"That's not the way it looked the night of Alicia's wedding reception. You looked pretty cozy to me."

"We just visited and talked about the good old days. He talked about was his art. You know how men are, their work, their cars, their sports. They can be so boring."

"I wouldn't mind being bored by Anthony Chadwick. He is gorgeous. Why didn't you two get married?"

"We were never that close. We were just friends."

"That's not how he felt. He told me one night how he was going to ask your father if he had his permission to marry you."

"What?" Elizabeth was shocked at Beth's revelation.

"You heard what I said. He didn't tell you about that?"

"Not a word, I had no idea."

"Elizabeth, you can't be serious. You had to know how he felt."

"I didn't. I am telling you the truth."

"Well, you missed out, wonder how the conversation went with your father?"

"I would imagine not well. Let's don't talk about this anymore."

"O.K. I have to get to work. Call me when you get a chance." Zoë said.

"Are you ready to go Beth?"

"Well, I was wondering how Anthony is doing. He said he was divorced?"

"Yes, but Karri is not interested in my old boyfriends. Let's go."

"You are wrong, I am very interested. This Anthony sounds fascinating to me. I want to hear more."

"There's nothing to tell. We were friends at university and he graduated, I still had another year before I graduated. We lost track of each other and that is the story."

"Karri, there is more but she doesn't want to talk about it, I think he'll be back. When he does, I promise I will let you know."

"Thank you, Beth sounds good to me." Karri winked at Beth.

"Let's go, I want to get my hair cut first then the spa. Is that all right with you Sherlock and Watson?"

# Chapter Nine

David whistled as he dressed for the day that he'd look forward to for such a long time. Finally, his waiting was over and he was going to Cambridge. He couldn't dress fast enough.

"Good morning Mrs. Waverly, how are you today?" David asked cheerfully going into her kitchen domain.

"I am doing wonderfully well. Thank you for asking. You sound chipper this morning. What are you so happy about?"

"I am happy to finally be able to go to Cambridge. I am finally going to walk all around the campus. I am not going to miss anything. This is my dream come true."

"Why are you so interested in that university in particular?"

"Mrs. Waverly, my dad and Uncle Creighton went there."

"Don't forget that Elizabeth and Alicia did as well."

"That's right I forgot about them. See all the Rose family went there. What about my grandparents, did they go there?"

"Yes, your grandfather did. I'm not sure about your grandmother, I wasn't very close to her she was a quiet lady and didn't talk much. Seems the men in the family were the ones that did the talking. What do you want for breakfast? "She laughed.

"I want the full English breakfast."

"Are you sure? Have you seen how much food that is? I don't mind, but I don't want to put you in shock when you see it. "

"I won't go into shock, I'm sure. I wanted to tell you how much I love your cooking. I dread the day we leave and I have to go back home."

"You are so welcome; you will have to come back often. I know Elizabeth would love for you to be here as much as you'd want."

"Thank you, I have to get back to school in August, so I have until then to enjoy my homeland." David said sighing as the regretful feelings of returning to California grew stronger with each day that he was in London.

"That's right, you were born here and Karri too. You were toddlers when you left. Do you remember much of your life before you left?"

"Not much, I vaguely remember my mother. How soft and kind she was. Did you know her?"

"I met her but I didn't really know her. She was beautiful. Karri reminds me of her. You look like your father, but I'm sure he has told you that."

"Yes, he has. He never remarried he said because he loved her so much and no one could ever take her place. He just threw himself into his business and has made it a success. I hope he will find someone someday that will start his motor running." He laughed.

"Me too. A man as handsome and nice as your father should be married. Share his life with someone and enjoy the life he has worked so hard to create."

"I have to meet him in the dining room; I just wanted to have a chance to talk to you and thank you for all the work you do to make us feel so at home here."

"They will bring you your breakfast when it's ready. So, remember, don't go in shock when you see it my lady." She laughed.

"Hi Dad, did you sleep well? You look a little tired."

"No, I haven't been able to get the journals out of my mind. They are haunting me. Creighton never once said anything about our father and mother being partial to me. I never once experienced it. He kept this all to himself. I wish I had known about it and I would have helped him get through it. Our lives were so far apart and never had the chance to have a relationship even if he did like me. I was totally clueless. How sad is that. I was living this happy go lucky life and he was drug down with rejection. But you know something? He made a very successful career. Did you know he was a barrister, the British attorney that can actually take cases to the courts? They are the ones that wear the wigs. Then he was an MP, a minister of Parliament. He did that even though he didn't have any support from his parents. I say support, I mean emotional support. They didn't love him or at least didn't show him love. I don't remember many times when I was with them that they showed me much love either. I never really thought about it much until it was brought to my attention through the journals. This has been a whole new outlook on life for me. I am sure I will never be the same."

"This is your breakfast, sir." The maid said as she pushed a large cart with enormous amounts of food on numerous plates to David's chair.

"What do you mean, all this? "

"Yes, sir, Mrs. Waverly told me to especially see that you ate every bit of it."

"David, what's this all about?"

"I told Mrs. Waverly I wanted the full English breakfast. I didn't know it included all this.'

"You might as well take your time and eat every bit of it, I know her and she will not forgive you if you don't, so just enjoy it, we will be here for a while." Timothy laughed at his son's surprised face and the time it was going to take him to eat his special order of the full English breakfast.

"Good morning, Uncle Timothy, David, how are you this morning?"

"Great." David said with his mouth full.

"Are you ready for our drive to Cambridge?"

"Yes, I am, I can't wait but I have to finish this monster of a breakfast first." He laughed.

"I see Mrs. Waverly has outdone herself."

"Uncle Timothy, I have been thinking about having a party. I wanted to invite some of your old friends and mine and some of our other members of the family. How does that sound to you?"

"Fine, I wouldn't mind seeing some friends I haven't seen since I left. I'll try to find them. When will you have it?"

"Next week. Friday night. Tell them eight o'clock. It will be formal, black tie. I am going to have an orchestra and everything. I want to celebrate a new life. A fresh start. I haven't done anything social in so long that I almost forgot how to be a hostess."

"Good for you Elizabeth. I like your hair, what did you do?"

"I just had it cut. Thank you."

"Hi everyone. Sorry I'm late; I was lazy and slept in." Karri said.

"Did you get your hair cut too?"

"Yes, Dad I did too. Elizabeth and I and Beth went to the spa as well. It was so wonderful. I can get used to this. I feel like a princess."

"You are my princess. You can go to a spa anytime you want when we get home. Just make the appointment when you want to."

"Oh, yeah Daddy's little 'tomboy' princess. All she wants to do is ride horses on the beach and read books." David chided his sister.

"What's wrong with that? It beats pretending you're Perry Mason."

"Perry Mason? What are you talking about?"

"Don't you remember we had to play 'courtroom' and you walked back and forth holding the lapels of your shirt like it was a jacket and spout off dumb things like, 'Did you see the accused ......' Whatever, I can't remember it all but you were a weird little kid." Karri laughed.

"Are we still going to Cambridge?" David asked changing the subject.

"Yes, we have to wait for David, uh, Perry, to shovel his way through the meal he ordered. We don't want him to be the accused, in Mrs. Waverly's court."

The four Roses talked and laughed as they ate their breakfast, and watched in awe as they focused on David and his endurance chocking down his colossal order from Mrs. Waverly.

"This is the most incredible day of my life." David said looking out the window when he saw the University of Cambridge sign.

"Can we just go anywhere we want, or do we have to be escorted by staff?"

"I think I can get a guest pass for you. I have to check to see what classes I need to take. I'll ask then. Just wait here and I'll be right back." Elizabeth said as they waited for her with Travis in the car.

"Tell me about all about, I don't know where to begin to ask questions."

"Well, the motto in Latin is: 'Hinc lucem et pocuta sacra'. The literal English translation we always used was *'From this place, we gain enlightenment and precious knowledge'*

It was established in 1209 and is a public university. Some of the famous alumni are: Isaac Newton, John Wallis, the inventor of Calculus and Darwin." Timothy shared some history of his alma mater.

"1209, you mean as in 1209? I don't know how to comprehend that date. They had students in 1209?" Karri tried to absorb the age of Cambridge."

"Karri, it's old. That's all, it's old. The motto is awesome; I need to write that down so I can remember it." David also tried to come to terms with the date of the founding of his dream school and the touching motto.

"Darwin. Did I hear you say Darwin? The one that said our ancestors were monkeys?" David asked.

"Yes, the same."

"That is such a bogus theory. I don't know about him, but not one of my pedigree charts show one ape or monkey. Now Karri, *he* was the *weird* one." David argued.

"Oh, I don't know, I think you both would be in good company." She laughed.

"David here is your guest badge and this is Eric Bolton, he will go with you and take you wherever you want to go. Have fun. Just phone Travis when you are ready to leave."

"I'm ready, and thank you Elizabeth. So, Eric let's go, I've waited for this all my life. See you all later."

"Glad that's finally over. He was driving me mad. Good riddance for the day." Karri sighed.

"Timothy, I have to meet my friends for lunch so why don't you and Karri come with me?"

"I don't see why not. Do you have anything Dad? You'll like her friends they are funny."

"No, I don't have plans. Lunch sounds ok to me; I'm just along for the ride. I have no agenda. "

Elizabeth used her new cell phone to call Beth and Zoë for the lunch place and time.

This lunch was at the Savoy where the friends wanted to meet for a special lunch to celebrate Zoë's promotion as head of her department at the BBC.

"I see them over there." Karris said.

"Hello, I want you both to meet Uncle Timothy, and this is Beth and Zoë."

"Glad to meet you, but I think I already have. It was at a lawn party during the summer just before I left for America. That was a long time ago."

"How long are you staying in London?" Beth asked.

"It just depends on Karri and David; I'm just along for the ride. They wanted to get acquainted with Elizabeth and Alicia and I agreed it was time our small family had a relationship and see where they were born."

"I hear you moved your business to America from here. Wasn't that difficult to re-establish there?"

"It was, but it was good for me. After my wife died, I needed something to plunge into. It is doing very well now, and I can take trips like this. I have very competent staff. I hear Zoë; congratulations are in order for your job promotion. I always admired the BBC with the choice programs they've made through the years. Our American PBS was good enough to bring them to us. "

"I have respect for them too. They are not perfect but their shortcomings haven't been an issue with me. I really like my job and this promotion will be a way I can implement some of my ideas, if they accept them."

"Good for you Zoë, you have a job where you can use your talents. You know, out of the three of us, you are the successful one. We always teased you about being an airhead, but in the end, you got the last laugh, didn't you?" Elizabeth said.

"I wouldn't say the last laugh, and I knew you both cared for me and loved to tease me so it was all right with me. I wouldn't trade either one of you for a barrel of monkeys."

"So, Elizabeth you need to complete the classes you need to teach and Beth, what about you?" Timothy asked.

"Since my divorce I haven't done very much. I need to go to work, but I'm not sure what I want to do. My children are in school and I want to make sure I am home when they are."

"What type of job are you looking for?" He wanted to know.

"My degree in the same as Elizabeth's, Art History. I can't teach because of the hours. So, I may go back and try something else."

"Are you ready to order?" The waiter asked.

Timothy found the company of his cousin and her friends very interesting and became more emotionally involved than he'd ever anticipated.

# Chapter Ten

The morning sun penetrated the turquoise water in the rectangle Olympic sized swimming pool where Timothy had decided to do some laps. When still at home this had been the routine in the summer, he would complete ten laps before breakfast.

He was feeling he had entered a renewed life, and this return home had been cathartic in every way. It allowed his children to restore their British heritage, David could make his wish come true to visit Cambridge, and then he had discovered the truth about his most esoteric brother.

"Good morning, David. How was your day, rather your day and night at Cambridge?" Timothy asked drying off.

"You can't even picture, I was in heaven. Dad, I need to talk to you. Please hear everything I have to say before you say no."

"All right, I'll listen." He said sitting down for breakfast.

"O.K., well, I want to move here and go to Cambridge and take International Law." He said as fast as he could before his father stopped him.

"You what?"

"You heard me, I want to move here and take International Law at Cambridge."

"I don't know what to say David, this is a total shock. You will have to let me think about it."

"Dad, I really don't need your permission, I'm an adult now, you know."

"That's true, you don't need my permission, I didn't mean to treat you like a child, I guess I just meant that I needed time to think about this, of course you can do what you want. This has been your dream as far back as I can remember and why it was such a shock to hear you say it just now, I don't know for you only brought it into reality."

"So, Dad, I can stay? I don't have to go back to Stanford?"

"Of course, you can stay. Where would you live?"

"There are places in Cambridge I could rent. We could go there today and see them. Could we do that Dad?"

"I don't see why not, so, International law? That sounds like a very difficult course. Are you able to qualify for it?"

"I don't have everything, but Eric helped me find the staff I needed to help me get organized with what I have and what I need before I can. I need a year to be eligible. They said my grades were good enough and since I am British, that plus my Uncle had been an MP, and of course both you and Uncle Creighton were alumni."

"You have it all sorted out. I am proud of you. This is happening so fast. Are you sure you want to live here? It is a lot different than L.A."

"I know and I love it. I love the slower pace and the more down to earth people that are here. I feel at home. I'm so glad you kept our British citizenship and did the dual citizenship. I want to be British. I am British. This is my home and I have always known I wanted to return for good."

"You don't even want to go back after graduation and live in L.A. what about Sarah?"

"I phoned her last night and she will be coming here as well. She can finish her architect degree here too; she and her father are on it now. We want to get married. Her mother said if she gave her consent that we would have to get married. We said yes."

"Married too? I don't' know if I can handle all this. Cambridge, moving here and now getting married. I just went into another world. I'm stunned, I knew you and Sarah were serious, and so did Karri. She will be over the moon, she likes Sarah, and they had become good friends. Sounds like we have a win, win situation here. Now where are you going to get married? Did you get that far with your sudden plans?"

"I am going to ask Elizabeth about having it here at Roselyn, what you think about that. Weren't you and mother married here?"

"Yes, we were."

"Do you think she will allow us to have the wedding and reception here?"

"You have to ask her, but I don't see any objection coming from her, she's delighted we are forming a family after all these years. "

"Good, I hoped I had it right, I felt it too that she was happy we were here, she was so glad I wanted to see England and be part of it again. I want to open an international law office here, but I can help with your company from here, so you see, I could come in handy."

"You could come in handy, is that anyway for an international attorney to talk?"

The father continued to help make the sudden plans that would carry his son completely away from him; he was already feeling the emptiness of losing his only son to Britain.

# Chapter Eleven

Elizabeth filled out a resume' while finishing her breakfast.

Since she was the first one downstairs and didn't know what the others had planned for the day she decided to get some paperwork done for job openings and brush up classes that would start in August and also share the good news about David with Beth.

"Beth, are you busy? I need to fill you in on David and his plans."

'What's going on?"

"We are going to have a wedding, and not only that but David is going to Cambridge to study international law."

"Really? I'm not surprised though the way Timothy was talking. I thought it would be nice for him to graduate from the same university his father and ancestors have for generations. What about a wedding, who's getting married?"

"David, and his girlfriend, Sarah. They did turn out to be more than just friends. Karri tried to tell me they were serious but he wouldn't let her. So, they are getting married and both will attend Cambridge to finish their degrees. The courses here will be inspiring for her enroll in the classes needed to complete her degree. He is so excited. I really love him. He feels more like a nephew than a cousin. I love Karri too. They are wonderful. Timothy did a good job being the mother and father."

"Yes, he is awesome." Beth sighed.

"What was that sigh for? Why Beth St. John, do you have a crush on my Uncle?"

"Don't be silly, I don't ever want another man in my life, well, not now anyway." She laughed trying to lead Elizabeth away from her feelings for Timothy that had emerged.

"I need you and Zoë to help me with the engagement party and wedding. The dinner Friday night can be turned into an engagement party.

Sarah and her parents will be here tomorrow. I can barely get ready for that, but it is good timing. They want to help them get settled in Cambridge. They want to buy a little cottage for their wedding present. Hope they know how expensive the real estate is there, but they will soon find out,

I don't want to interfere. I guess Sarah's father and Timothy have been friends for years."

"I can imagine Timothy will miss David. They are so close. I feel sorry for him, but he and Karri are close too, so that is good." Beth said.

"Yes, they are all three closes. I never thought about Karri and Timothy going back alone. It is all happening so fast. But that is life, isn't it?"

"Yes, that is life and things do happen quickly and unexpected."

"What do you mean by that?"

"Oh, nothing, just agreeing with you on the sudden and unexpected things that happen in life."

"Can you come over and help me get started on the plans?"

"Sure, I'll be there shortly."

Beth was a very attractive woman with her glossy dark brown hair and bright blue eyes and could at times be stunning, especially when she was happy.

Since her divorce, her countenance had changed into a drab and dull mother of twin boys aged five, and had been barely able to survive each depressing day.

Her family trust had allowed her to live in the large estate and stay at home with the children and with the help of a nanny, a cook, housekeeper and a maid and assorted staff, she was able to survive.

Her parents died when she was very young and she vaguely remembered them. She had been raised by her father's parents. They were also an old British family on the same level of society as the Rose family, she, like Elizabeth had no brothers so she inherited the family trust. She had made sure her twins would be her heirs, even though they hadn't possessed the family name making the old outdated trust include her sons.

"Miss Elizabeth is by the pool, Miss Beth; I'll take you to her." Hodges said opening the door for her.

"Thank you, Hodges, are you ready for all the big plans?" Beth asked.

"We will have to get organized, won't we?"

"Hi Liz, are you ready to plan?"

"Yes, I think I am, I have just sent in the forms for university and now I can concentrate on the wedding. I am getting excited."

"Good for you, we can use some excitement in our lives, can't we? Good grief... I didn't know he was here."

Beth paused as she saw Timothy climb out of the pool.

"Hi Beth. Good to see you again. How are you?" He asked grabbing a towel.

"I'm fine....fine."

"Have you heard the good news about David and Sarah?"

"Yes, that's why I'm here to help Liz with the plans. That is, if it's ok with you for me to help.....I mean...."

"Of course, we will all need your help. There is so much to do. Sarah will be here tomorrow with her parents. I guess the dinner party Friday will turn into an engagement party, that was good timing, wasn't' it?"

"Yes, it was." Beth agreed with him as her heart beat wildly. The first day she'd seen him since his return she'd been surprised at her reaction. She could feel warm emotions for this man come to the surface, but she instantly pushed them away and wouldn't allow herself to even think about this young uncle of her friend to be more than just approval of how he looked, especially now climbing out of the pool drenched with water and looking all tan and......she stopped her thoughts at that instant and would never let that happen again. He was just an ordinary man. An uncle of her friend.

"Beth, are you O.K.?" Elizabeth asked Beth.

"Yes, I just had some things on my mind I forgot to do before I left home. I need to call and remind Jennifer, the twin's nanny I won't be home until later."

102

Beth said quickly guiding them in another direction of her thoughts than the ones she was actually thinking.

"Let's get planning. I know we have to consult Sarah's mother on things, but we can at least alert the florist, caterers, but most of all our household staff. "

"Karri, hello, did you sleep in again?" Elizabeth asked.

"I did, I don't know what it is about this place but I can really sleep. It must be the mammoth feather bed." She laughed.

"I wanted to tell you, we have stables, and did you see them? You can ride anytime you like. When David told us about how you liked to ride horses on the beach, I was going to tell you then, but I must have lost my train of thought. Sorry about that."

"Are you kidding me?"

"No, she isn't, we had lots of horses didn't I ever tell you about that?" Timothy asked.

"You never did tell me any such thing. I would have never forgotten, Dad, you never talked about Roselyn. You always would say, that is in the past and 'I don't' want to be reminded of anything about it.' So we didn't. " Karri lamented.

"I know, that was not fair was it? I deprived you of knowing anything your heritage, I'm sorry, maybe I can make it up to you now."

"I'm going to the stables; do you need me for anything?"

"No, I think we can manage." He laughed.

"Thank you, Elizabeth, for allowing my children to feel at home here. I will always appreciate it. You have been wonderful."

"Timothy, this your home too. I'm sorry my father was so insensitive to you and David and Karri and was the instrument that made you move from your home. You could have brought them here to live if he hadn't been so morose."

"I know, I'd even thought about that, but I also think things work out for the best, I made my company into something that was mine, not the Rose family name. Today that is a good feeling. I do want my children to enjoy all they can from their heritage though. With your help I know they will have that chance now."

"No question about that." Elizabeth smiled.

"Now, let's plan a wedding. "Beth said trying not to focus on Timothy.

"By the way I saw Anthony yesterday; I forgot to phone you last night. I saw him in London; he was driving a little black sports car. Did you know he was back?"

"No, what makes you think I care if he is here or in Paris, or where ever he lives."

"Sorry, did I touch a sore spot?"

"No, not at all, I just don't know why you insist that we have a relationship other than acquaintances and that we don't keep tabs on each other's whereabouts."

"Me thinks the lady does protests too much..." Timothy laughed.

"I agree. She forgets I was there when they were going together, well whatever she wants to call it. He even told me he was going to ask her father if he could marry her."

"I told you I didn't know about that. Did he ever tell you what happened when he talked to father?"

"Oh, now she's letting her guard down, we got her interest. Yes, he did tell me all about it. He was devastated the next day when he told me Mr. Rose ordered him off his property and he was never allowed to come back. He'd said that he didn't want any useless artist from Cornwall to ever see his daughter again."

"My father said that?"

"He did, isn't that sad?"

"I am sorry; I need to apologize to Anthony. Do you have his phone number?"

"Yes, I do, I just happen to have it here in my phone directory." Beth said smiling at her success in getting Elizabeth interested in calling her long lost suitor.

"Beth, what do you do to fill your life other than your children?"

"Not a lot. I am going to take some more art history classes with Elizabeth when she goes back though. I may find something to do in that area. Anyway, it will get some of the cobwebs out and also have some fun with my long-lost friend."

"How would you like to take a drive to Brighton with me today? I can't do anything after tomorrow. I'd like to get out and see some of my favorite places before Karri and I leave."

"Sounds good to me, Elizabeth, do you need me for anything else?"

"No, I have everything under control now, until tomorrow anyway." She smiled thinking about Timothy and Beth.

"I need to go home first, do you mind?"

"No, that's fine, I need to rent a car on the way, is that ok?"

"You don't have to do that. I have my car with me and we can take it, if that's ok with you. You can drive, I mean, if you want."

"Good, that will save time and I would like to drive. Let me change clothes. I'll be right back."

"Beth, do I detect a relationship forming?"

"Just because we're going for a drive to Brighton?"

"No, just because I feel pounding hearts that will be driving to Brighton."

She laughed.

"Pounding hearts. What a thing to say. Pounding hearts. You sound like a character in a Jane Austen book."

"We'll see, you just remember I told you so..."

"You are very funny, now you get on the phone and call Anthony to see what he is doing."

Beth laughed as she hugged Elizabeth good bye.

"Have a good day you two." She said as she watched her best friend and very young-looking uncle leave for a long drive to the south of England.

"Hi Anthony, this is Elizabeth, I needed to talk to you, I didn't know you were in town, Beth just told me. Could you come over?"

"I have some business to take care of first. I'm not too thrilled about meeting you there though, let's have lunch at Paddy's, one o'clock, how does that sound?"

"O.K., I'll meet you at one o'clock at Paddy's."

Elizabeth hurried upstairs to her bedroom thinking once again she needed to redecorate. The wedding would be the perfect excuse. She quickly dialed the designer she knew from several years before and asked for them to come out tomorrow and help her decide what she wanted done to make her bedroom livable and come to life as she was.

Anthony waited for Elizabeth thinking about their last angry departure. He was sorry for his impatient manner with her. He wasn't as secure as he had been when he was younger. There had been so many painful memories with his ex-wife, who couldn't be satisfied with him for a husband; she had to try to conquer every man she came in contact with. This phenomenal experience left him cold and bitter. When Elizabeth started her usual prattle that day, they were going to Cornwall he found to his surprise that he didn't have the patience to forge through the forest of words to get to the heart of a meaningful conversation with her that day. Now he was glad to have the opportunity to apologize.

"Sorry I'm late, but we have so many things going on now I had to do some phoning before I left and it took longer than I thought."

"That's all right. I 'm in no hurry, I was thinking about our last time together and I wanted to apologize for the abrupt manner I took you home, I'm really sorry."

"That's O.K., no harm done. As a matter of fact, I wanted to apologize to you."

"You mean for telling me I was a jerk?" He laughed.

"No, I'll tell you later, let's order. I'm hungry. "She wanted to prolong the ensuing emotions that would occur when she would reveal her new discovery about her father's treatment of him, so long ago.

The waiter took their order and the pair avoided eye contact. They looked around the old familiar pub and restaurant trying to find comfort under the uncomfortable circumstances.

"Why are you in London?"

"I have a showing in a couple of weeks. It takes time to get things organized and invitations sent out. There are also the politics involved."

"Politics, in art?"

"Yes, in art if you can believe it. I don't want to go into it, but trust me there is. Now tell me what have you been doing? Is Alicia and Jordan back from their honeymoon?"

"No, in fact I just heard from her yesterday and they are extending it until August. They met some friends in Athens and they decided to go back to the continent and go to Italy for the rest of their trip."

"That's some trip. Guess there would be lots to see though since they have the time and aren't working."

"I am happy for them; this took some endurance for them to wait until father passed away before they could get married."

"What do you mean, wait until he died. I thought he liked Jordan and his family."

"He did, but he wouldn't let them get married until he died. Jordan argued with him many nights about it, but nothing could change his mind. My father would tell him off many times and I was always surprised when he'd come back. I guess that proved he loved Alicia to go through all that, for so long."

"I guess it did. Jordan must be a strong person to have taken the abuse. Your father was not an easy person."

"No, he wasn't. He was the cause of many lives torn apart. Someday I will elaborate."

"I am going to Cornwall before the show; would you like to try once again, that is if I can behave myself, to go with me?"

"When? I have things coming up tomorrow and Friday. We are having an engagement party for David, Timothy's son. Would you like to come? It is a sudden wedding. He has decided to stay here and to Cambridge for his international law degree and that brought on the wedding."

"I think so; I can't see any reason why I couldn't be there. Black tie?"

"Yes, black tie. We want to do the best we can for the couple, they are starting a totally new and different lifestyle. Her parents are buying them a cottage close to the university for their wedding gift. So they should be comfortable while they finish their degrees."

"Sounds like Timothy's life is changing. He will miss his son I'm sure. "

"He will, but he has a daughter too, Karri, she will go back with him and continue  her degree at Stanford."

"Did you say you were going to finish your degree so you can teach?"

"I just sent the forms back today as a matter of fact. Beth is going to go back for some refresher courses with me. It will be like old times."

"What about Zoë?"

"She just got a promotion and is the head of her advertising department at the BBC. We also found out there is someone in her life now. We didn't know until the lunch we had to celebrate her promotion. I guess they are serious and looks like a wedding there in the near future."

"Everyone is getting married. Like dominos, isn't it?"

"I guess so." Elizabeth sighed.

The couple relived their past for the rest of the afternoon while he took her for a long drive after their lunch.

Elizabeth was finally able to work up the courage to apologize for her father's behavior when he'd ask him if he could marry her.

Anthony didn't want to discuss it and promptly said it was all right then changed the subject.

"Will you be able to go to Cornwall with me next week?"

"I'm sorry, I have the engagement party this week and then the wedding the next. I have other classes I have to go to as well. I won't be able to go."

"That's all right. Maybe another time."

"Yes, maybe another time."

She was certain her father's rejection of him had been a very deep wound and she felt a deep remorse for him to have gone through that ordeal alone, but it did explain a lot about his sudden departure to Paris.

# Chapter Twelve

Elizabeth was glad the engagement party and wedding were behind her, and David and Sarah were on their honeymoon in Rome.

Karri didn't miss David as much as she'd thought. She was so busy with the horses that she was allowed to help take care of by walking them and taking turns riding them all to make sure they all had their exercise. She was in heaven.

Elizabeth's renovation of her bedroom was completed; it was now fresh with new rose floral material that covered the windows, bed and cushions of her loveseat and dressing table chair cover. This was what she had wanted for years but her father said that a rose color was too much rose for him, meaning Rose for their surname was all the roses he wanted in his home.

She had them paint her fireplace white which made the rose floral chintz even crispier and fresher.

She was happy for the first time in many years to be able to concentrate on what she wanted to do. The things she had contemplated for years that she'd wanted to try.

"Miss Elizabeth, your driver is here." Miss Pendle said as she tapped on her door.

"Thank you, I'll be there in just a minute, well maybe two." She laughed.

The driver that was waiting for her was her driving instructor.

She was going to drive. Tired of having to call Travis each time she wanted to go somewhere, it would be nice just to hop in the car and go.

She peered at the little man while he was telling her how to prepare before you actually started the car. He had a pinched face that told her he was already stressed. This was not a good sign she thought. 'I don't want to start out with this guy already uptight, but I don't have a choice.

So, she took a deep breath and proceeded with his instructions about the mirrors, seatbelt and to be sure to watch both ways before pulling onto the street.'

"Go slowly, you'll be fine. Remember a car length behind the car in front of you." He said confidently.

He said as he jotted some notes on his clipboard.

"O.K., good, now let's stay in this lane for now. Just keep following the car ahead."

"What if he turns?"

"Well, don't; please don't turn if he turns."

"O.K., then just follow him if he keeps going straight but if he turns I won't follow. Is that right?"

"Yes, that's correct."

She thought he was a little 'toffee nose', as she and Beth used to make fun of someone like him who tried to be a perfectionist and was pompous.

"Slow down just a bit. Remember keep a car length between you and the car you are following."

"That is unless he turns, is that right?"

"Yes, Miss, that is right." He agreed losing some of his confident air.

Elizabeth was going to have a little fun with him and she couldn't wait to tell Beth about him.

"Now, let's turn left at the next corner, what will you do before you turn?"

"I don't know, we haven't gotten that far. What do I do?" She laughed to herself.

"You're right, I didn't' tell you what to do. So, let's don't turn. Wait until I tell you what to do then we'll turn." He took a deep breath.

"O.K., so I keep following the car ahead, one car length behind because I don't know what to do to turn left yet, is that correct?"

"Yes, that is right." He cleared his throat and straightened up in his seat.

"O.K., now, to make a left turn you need to signal. Do you know how to use the turn signal lever?" He asked her with a condescending attitude.

"No, I don't. What do I do?"
"Grasp the lever with your right hand."

"Like this?" She gripped the lever tightly purposely making her words and jesters slow and simple.

"Well not quite that tight. Relax a little."

"Like this?" She said having a hard time not laughing out loud at him and his change of demeanor to this squeaky little man that was having a hard time being patient with her and answer her questions.

"You need to hold it lightly, not tightly. Like this. He pushed he hand away and held the lever for her getting edgy with her.

"Now, holding the turn signal lever lightly, go ahead, hold it lightly and push up to turn left and down to signal you are going to turn right.

"Push up to turn left, like this?"

"Not yet. Not yet." He yelled. "We're not quite ready to turn."

"Oh, I see, I wait until I'm ready to turn before I use the turn signal. "

"That's right. Wait until we're ready to actually turn."

"Now you be sure to tell me when we are ready to actually turn so, I'll know what to do..." She bit her lip not to smile.

"That's right, just do as I tell you and we will be just fine. Now, see the corner ahead of the car in front of you?"

"You mean the car I'm to follow unless he turns then I keep going straight?"

"Yes, that's the one. Well, when you get to the corner engage your turn signal and turn left."

"So, I, now what? Engage? What does that mean?"

"PUSH. Engage means PUSH; it's as simple as that. JUST PUSH THE LEVER."

"O.K. Push the lever, oops. I just passed the corner I was going to turn left on, what do I do now?"

"Just wait until we get to the next corner then push the lever and turn left." He said taking a deep breath and reached for his handkerchief.

"Got it."

"Very good, Miss. Now let's follow this car ahead, remember the car length behind, then we are going to maneuver to the inside lane. Remember we are in a round-a-bout and we must watch for the 'out' we want to take."

" Out?"

"Yes, out, or exit which ever you want to call it. So we will take the 'out' or exit to Croydon, do you see that on the sign?"

"No, I didn't."

"That's all right, let's go around again and then you look up and see the sign that says Croydon, O.K.?"

'Yes, I go around until I see the sign that says Croydon."

"Then what?" He asked trying to mask his frustration with her.

"What do you mean then what? I don't know, you just said to go around until I see the sign that says Croydon, that's all you said, I don't know what to do after that." She was trying so hard not to burst out laughing. She started coughing to cover her laughing for getting him so upset on purpose.

"Sorry, you're right; I didn't tell you what to do when you saw the sign. So, when you see the sign... you missed seeing it again. Now, let's go around once more. When we see the sign to Croydon, see when you want to change lanes to be sure we can take the proper 'out'. .er. .exit." He said as fast as he could before they got to the sign again so she could see what exit she needed to take.

By this time she was in quite hysterics.

"Now what do we do when we see the sign to Croydon?"

"I still don't know. You haven't' told me, we haven't' gotten that far." She was doing all she could not to double over.

"Let's just relax" He took another deep breath. "Now, when we see the sign to Croydon, we will maneuver the car over into the lane that will take us to the exit we want to go to take. O.K? Got that?" He asked sharply.

"Yes, yes, I think I do." She repeated what he just said.

"Now, do you see the Croydon sign?" He asked her as they went around the round-a-bout for the *fifth* time trying to see the sign and prepare to exit.

"Yes, I see it. I see it. Now I go into what lane? *Just tell me what lane* and I will go there you snooty little man." She couldn't hold it back any longer.

"I have been telling you and you won't listen. All you do is keep repeating everything I say."

"I have to try to understand what you're telling me to do. Just tell me what lane and I will get in the lane, I don't care if it's Croydon, or Exeter, just tell me, what lane."

"You're getting upset now, so we must remain calm or you will have an accident."

By this time, it was too late; Elizabeth had crossed into a lane too close to a car and hit him.

They stopped. Both the student driver and the instructor were letting off as much steam as the crashed vehicles were.

The traffic slowed to a stop on the round-a-bout that Elizabeth could never find the proper lane to get into and get to the exit to Croydon.

The cars weren't as frayed as their nerves were. The large 'L', white sign, alerting everyone that there was a Learner' driving the car, on the front and back of the driving school's car, and were dangling at an angle from the sudden impact.

"Elizabeth, are you all right?"

She heard a familiar voice. It was Anthony.

"Yes, I'm fine, just frustrated from driving around in circles trying to find the proper 'out', or whatever they call it."

"I saw you about two circles ago and wondered what you were doing so I followed you. Glad I didn't miss the show. You looked so funny. I could tell you didn't know how to get to the exit." He laughed. "I thought there for a while you were going to make some butter. Remember the children's story about the tiger that ran in circles until he made butter?" He kept laughing at her enjoying the predicament he'd just by a lucky happenstance found her in.

"Leave me alone. You are not the least bit funny. You always did made fun of me at the most awkward times. I just want to get out of this car. Can you take me home?"

"Sure, when they get here to record the accident, just sit in my car and I'll wait here for you."

The ride to Roselyn was quiet. Elizabeth was still fretting about the accident she had caused and the little man's attitude and the report he gave the policeman that she was totally out of control when she'd driven into the lane where she'd hit the car.

"You know it's not the end of the world. It was a very minor accident and a very common one, they happen every day. This one just happened to be you and no one was injured." He tried to lighten her mood.

"I don't ever want to drive again. I want to tell Travis when and where I want to go and be done with it. No more driving for me. That ...that... pretentious little man. He couldn't teach anyone anything. I don't know how he keeps his job."

"Now, now, Lizzie, calm down, you can't give up that easy, this was only your first day driving. I know he was just trying to do his job. I can imagine you were not very helpful, were you?"

'Well, I guess not." She smiled.

"He was so precise, snooty and condescending I couldn't help myself. I did mock him by repeating everything he said." She started laughing and didn't stop until they reached Roselyn.

"Thank you, Tony; I was so grateful to see you at the accident."

"That's the first time you've called me that since, well, since I've been back. Does this mean you'll go to Cornwall with me?"

"Yes, when do you want to go? I'm free until I start classes next month."

"Good, how about tomorrow, shall we try once more? Will you ask Mrs. Waverly to fix our lunch again?" He smiled.

"I can do that, of course she will be happy you asked. She wanted to know what happened last time and I was so upset I couldn't tell her, but I'm sure she'll be glad to have another chance and I promise this time to behave and act like a grown up, well, let's say I will try to act like a grown up, I don't know about behaving."

"At least you're being honest. I have *never* seen you behave. That was one thing I could count on. I suppose it must come from the rebellion of your father's control and when you were away from him you utilized your freedom to the fullest." He laughed as he opened her car door and looked down at her as he relished the sweetness she could portray when she wanted.

"I am sure you're right. I thought when I was away from him no one could tell me what to do, and then you'd try to boss me." She stood up and gave him a kiss.

He held her and kissed her the way he did when they were younger. She pulled away and took a deep breath.

"You haven't lost it, Tony. You can still knock my socks off. I shouldn't tell you that though, you'll get a swelled head." She laughed remembering how they used to tease each other and then end up in passionate kisses then they would quickly say good night.

"Oh, yeah, well I see you still have them on." He laughed.

"See you in the morning; do you want to have breakfast here? Mrs. Waverly would be over the moon if you did. I'll tell her you will, ok?"

"I guess so. See you about, oh, how about nine o'clock?"

"Good, see you then." She ran through the massive wooden double doors.

# *Chapter Thirteen*

Timothy leisurely ate breakfast by the pool as he read the London Times. He'd forgotten how much he enjoyed British newspapers. When he returned home, he would order subscriptions.

"Hi Karri, have you had breakfast?"

"No, I'm starved."

"Good, we need to talk about going home, I wanted to get back and do some work with the new clients I've found here. It is amazing how the business gets a life of it's own and can't get out of it. I can see why it was easier to have my company here than at home. I think we should make reservations for next week, what do you think?"

"Dad, I don't want to go back. I had a long talk with Elizabeth and she said I could live here with her. I could stay at Cambridge during the week and come home on weekends. What do you think?"

Timothy was astonished at her news. He had never thought about her staying in England as well.

"I don't like the idea of losing both my children at the same time. Can't I persuade you to go back with me? Why can't you go to school at Stanford?"

"No, I want to stay here and I know what courses I want to take. I want to be a vet."

"You mean an animal doctor?"

"Yes, Dad, an animal doctor." She repeated sarcastically.

"Guess there's nothing I can say is there? What am I going to do without my little buttercup?"

"Dad, you promised you would never call me that name again."

"Sorry, it just slipped out. So, guess I will make my reservations for next week. "

He couldn't say any more. His heart was broken. He hadn't felt this kind of pain since his wife passed away. He was stunned.

The father and daughter quietly finished their meal and Karri rushed off to the stables.

Emptiness shrouded him like an iron suit. He starred at the paper trying to get his emotions under control. The thoughts of leaving both children in London and he would have to go home alone ran through his mind along with the question of how was he going to survive?

"Hello, Beth, yes, yes, I can make it. I'll see you in a little while, glad you called." He hung up from her call thinking about his lonely trip home.

Timothy drove to Beth's estate located a few kilometers from Roselyn.

She had been in a similar situation Elizabeth and Alicia had grown up in, with the exception of her father that was not a morose man, he was jovial and her mother also. They'd passed away just after her divorce so she had been in mourning for three important people in her life all at the same time.

"Hi Timothy." Beth said cheerfully standing in front of her butler. "I had an idea and wanted to see if you wanted to come along with me."

"What's this idea?" He asked as she walked him to the back of the estate to the pool area. "Peter, we'll have some lemonade."

"Yes, Miss."

The pool was oval shaped filled with bright blue water that accented the porous adobe-colored tiles that surrounded it.

The orange umbrellas shaded the large wooden tables and chairs that coordinated with the chaise lounges that were carefully placed around the large pool.

"Now, what is this idea of yours?" He asked thankful for her rescue.

"I wanted to take a trip to Florence to review the museums there for some of the classes I'm going to be taking next month. I thought you might like to join me. I hate to travel alone. Everyone else is occupied with either work or can't be talked into it. So, I thought you might enjoy a trip to the continent before you went back home. Would Karri be interested in coming along as well?"

"I don't think she would, did you hear about her new plans to stay here"

"Yes, I did. Elizabeth told me. I'm sorry. I know you must feel abandoned."

"I do, that is the exact feeling, abandoned."

"So, what do you think? Would you like to go?"

"You are talking about Florence, Italy?"

"That would be the one."

"When will you be going and how long will you be gone?"

"I can leave whenever the time is right for you and I will come back when you need to get back. It will be on your schedule."

"How can I say no? Let me do some business, I found some new clients here and that shouldn't take but a day, so we could leave day after tomorrow? Will you make the reservations? Since I'm able to take care of the new business I can extend my trip here and let them carry on at home, they have been doing a wonderful job, so far. So, it's up to you how long we stay."

"Good, I wanted to make it open ended and not put a date on coming back. We may want to go to Rome as well. I haven't been there since school days. It feels good to get back into the swing of things."

"That's settled, here's to the trip and getting back into the swing of things and may we enjoy the hell out of it." He said lifting his glass of lemonade into the air with a toast to their trip.

"Mommy, we want to go for a swim, Jennifer said we had to ask you, may we?"

Beth's five-year-old dark haired twin boys ran out to meet their mother. The tender relationship was evident to Timothy and almost moved him to tears, thinking about David and Karri at that age.

"Ashton and Brandon, I want you to meet Timothy Rose. Timothy, these are my son's."

"Nice to meet you, Ashton and Brandon, now which is which?"

"I am Ashton, I have the freckles on my nose and that is Brandon he doesn't."

"Oh, so let me get this straight. You are Ashton, you have freckles on your nose and this is Brandon and he doesn't have freckles on his nose, is that correct?"

"You got it."

"Mommy, can we go for a swim? Jennifer told us to ask you.

"Go tell her you can swim, but we won't need her, I think Timothy and I will join you, is that all right with you?"

"Sure, do you have extra suits?" He asked.

"No, we're going 'skinny dipping'." Beth laughed at him.

"You are funny." He said smiling enjoying her sense of humor.

"You can go change, you can see the white adobe changing rooms and I'll be back in a few minutes."

The pool came alive with splashing and giggling. The boys loved the water and had several games they liked to play. Timothy and Beth joined them in their fun where the abandoned father's emptiness faded away.

# *Chapter Fourteen*

The azure water shimmered on the Cornish coast from the sun. Its rays penetrated through the depths of the water and uncovered the beautiful sea creatures that gathered there.

The seagulls perched high on the mounds of rocks waited for their prey to surface.

Each summer the round of the food chain was the same revealing the renewal from winter's hibernation and the continuing flow of seasons and nature, one not more important than the other.

Man, birds and fish all linked together in this exquisite land that was culminated on the southern shores of England.

Each summer the cycle of the food chain was the same, revealing the summer's renewal from winter's hibernation and the continual flow of seasons and nature, one not more important than the other.

Man, birds and fish all linked together in this exquisite land, the southern shores of England.

"This incredible country always inspires me. I always have the feeling that the pirates from Penzance will jump off their ships docked in the bay and start singing the music from Gilbert and Sullivan. Do you ever think about that?"

"Not once. You are strange, Elizabeth Ann Rose. For such a highbrow. Where do you come up with those ideas? I've lived here all my life and never once have I had that thought."

"Well, what thoughts do you have? Mr. Anthony Paul Chadwick."

"Let me see, what thoughts do I have, well today I have been thinking how nice you have been on this trip. You haven't cussed anyone out, you haven't insulted anyone, and you have been as well behaved as any well-bred Londoner I've seen. Are you up to something?"

"Up to something? Why would I be up to something and what would I be up to?"

"Heaven only knows what you could be up to. I remember very clearly our school days. You, Beth and Zoë, were usually in the middle of something."

"You weren't around much then, because we were very studious and didn't have the time to be up to something."

"You, studious? I don't remember too many times I saw you even carry books."

"We did most certainly carry books, how could we go to classes without books?"

"That puzzled me too. How could you go to class without books?"

"Stop that. You sound like me when I was with my driving instructor the other day."

"Is that what you did to the poor little man?"

"I did." She started laughing.

"You are a menace, Miss Rose. I have your number; I know exactly what you are. You look and sound like a beautiful angelic woman, and at times remind me of a beautiful pink rose then Bang. You shoot yourself down with all the sarcastic rhetoric added to your combatant behavior. It was a shock the first time I truly got to know you. I saw this lovely rose suddenly wilt and huge thorns on its stem popped out."

"That was not very flattering. Alicia hasn't even said that to me. She just calls me 'bossy'."

"I guess she didn't want to hurt your feelings. But I found no one could hurt your feelings. With your acid tongue spewing out shocking remarks I knew you could take what you handed out." He laughed. "Yes, I had nightmares about you and your long whip like acid tongue, you know."

"Nightmares? You never said anything about having nightmares about me. What an awful thing to say." She folded her arms, closing him out.

"Sorry, I guess I went too far. Well, I guess they weren't nightmares, they were just dreams." He laughed trying to soften his remarks.

"How are your parents? Do they still have that beautiful bed and breakfast on the hill overlooking the ocean?" She asked changing the subject.

"They are doing very well, and they do have the bed and breakfast. I worry now that they should sell it and retire, but they don't want to, so not much I can do. It's their life."

"It's better for them to be active than to sit around and do nothing like some of the older people do in London. They are useless. I think that is sad, to be useless."

"Guess you're right. They are happy so that's the important thing."

"How have you been Tony?"

"All right, I guess. Busy running around with the art. It seems all I do is pack and unpack. But that is the nature of the game. This is what I wanted and this is what I got. Can't complain."

"Are you happy?"

'I suppose. I'm the happiest when I'm actually painting. But it all goes together. In order to paint you have to sell the stuff."

"You don't' sound too happy. There is an undercurrent there. What's that all about? Is it your ex-wife?"

"I don't know what you mean, an undercurrent. Are you going to therapy?"

"Yes, why?"

"You sound like a therapist asking me those questions."

"Sorry, just an observation, how far are we from St. Ives?"

'We should be there in about an hour."

The large bed and breakfast nestled on the emerald hill side absorbed the beauty from the surrounding of earth, water and sky highlighting its white edifice.

The spectacular view from the antique windows was breathtaking.

The couple drove up the long drive to the 'Chadwick Bed and Breakfast '.

Anthony was always happy to see the well-maintained place each time he returned. This was home. This was where he grew up, and The Tate Gallery in town was where he began his love of art.

"Elizabeth. We are so happy you could come. Anthony told us about your father and we are so sorry for your loss."

"Thank you, Mrs. Chadwick, for the invitation and the beautiful flowers you sent for the funeral."

"We were not able to go to the funeral. Our season was getting started in May so we couldn't get away."

"I understand. Your place is so lovely; I'd forgotten how beautiful it is."

"Thank you, we love it here and couldn't be happier."

"Hello, Elizabeth. How are you? How long has it been since you've been here?" Mr. Chadwick asked coming in from the garden.

"It must have been at least ten years ago, when my father fell ill."

"I didn't realize it was that long since you've been to see us. We will make up for lost time. Anthony you're not in a hurry to get back?"

"No, nothing pressing for about a month. Elizabeth is involved in some classes so I don't know how long she has."

"I'm free for a week, but I need to get back for the classes he was talking about. By the way, Mrs. Chadwick, I want your help with my roses. I need your advice. When we get the chance, I would like to see your gardens."

"Of course. We will have dinner at eight o'clock. The guest will eat at seven so we can have our privacy. Take your showers and we will have a walk in the garden."

The weary couple trudged up the spiral staircase to the bedrooms and grateful the long trip was over and now they could enjoy their trip that had not been interrupted by a quarrel this time.

The Chadwick dining room was not formal like the one in Roselyn but it was large enough to seat as many guests as the old bed and breakfast would need. The long heavy wooden table-built generations ago still shone its luster and could be set with the finest culinary design. The family crystal, china and silverware were delicate and after adding candles and flowers the ambience was as splendid as at Roselyn.

"I hope you don't mind but we invited Nigel for dinner."

"You what?" Anthony asked coming into the kitchen where his mother was giving orders to the cook.

"You heard what I said. I don't understand why you don't like him. He is very successful in his business and he is devastated about his last divorce." His mother shared with him.

"Yeah, his fourth divorce. He must be setting a record for solicitors. At least he saves money on his attorneys." Anthony sneered.

"Solicitors are attorneys. Now what is the matter with you? Nigel just had a run of bad luck with the ladies."

"Bad luck all right. His problem is he's never seen a female he didn't like."

"Hush, here he is."

"Good evening, Nigel, so good of you to come. Have a seat in the parlor we'll have dinner in an hour. "

"Hi Anthony, I haven't seen you in ages. How have you been?"

"Good, very good." He said hardly able to get the few words out.

He detested his cousin. They had grown up together but never had very much in common. He was his father's older brother's son and there had been a rivalry between the brothers which filtered down to the cousins.

Mrs. Chadwick felt it her duty to try to bring the men together but it so far, she had not had success.

"How long are you visiting this time? Don't you get tired of traveling?"

"I'm not sure how long I'll be here this time, Elizabeth has to be home by next week so guess I'll leave then and take her home."

"Elizabeth Rose?"

"Yes, she drove with me. You know her father passed away?"

"Yes, I did, but guess everyone was relieved according to my sources."

"Elizabeth. So good to see you after all these years. You must be doing well, you look incredible."

"Thank you, I didn't know you would be here. How have you been?"

"I could be better. I am just getting over my divorce."

"His fourth." Anthony muttered and took Elizabeth by the arm and sat her beside him on the love seat.

"I have some business in London in a couple of weeks, could I stop by and say hello while I'm there?"

"Of course, Nigel, just phone when you are in town."

"Don't answer when he does." Anthony whispered.

"What was that, Anthony?"

"Nothing I was just checking to see if you were comfortable."

"Yes, I am "She said after he put his arm around her shoulders and brought her closer to him letting Nigel know she was with him and to stay away from her.

"Elizabeth, you wanted to see the garden, we have time before we eat, let's take a walk." Mrs. Chadwick said.

"What is wrong with Anthony? He's acting funny and keeps muttering something under his breath?"

"Oh, don't pay any attention to him, he and Nigel don't get along too well, I try to bring them together once in a while but it always turns out this way. Anthony acts like a juvenile. "

The garden's variety of fragrances that early evening was intoxicating. Mother Nature had outdone herself. The roses were splendid and the other flowers enhanced their aroma, to Elizabeth's delight.

She and Mrs. Chadwick had been very fond of each other and it felt good to renew their friendship.

The two women entered the dining room where the men had already been seated.

The table was gleaming from the candles illuminating the antique crystal glasses, and freshly picked flowers from her garden. Mrs. Chadwick's effect was outstanding and had even seemed to warm the hearts of the battling cousins.

After Nigel left Anthony took Elizabeth for a walk outside to enjoy the ocean view from the deck.

They sat in the comfortable pastel yellow cushioned chairs that harmonized the chaise lounges and table cloths on the table with umbrellas.

"This is stunning. The water looks like glass from the reflection from the lights."

"It is, I never get tired of anything here, except, Nigel." Anthony laughed.

"Why can't you get along with him? He seems to be a nice man."

"He seems to be a lot of things, depends who you are and if you're a woman or not. He loves anything in a skirt."

"You don't like him I know, but what has he done to you? Just because he likes the ladies."

"You would have had to grow up with him to understand what I am talking about, and we don't have the time to cover even part of what a rat he truly is."

"No matter, I don't' care, whatever, you have to live your life and I can't choose your friends for you, even cousins." She laughed. "This is the first time I've seen you act like this. Talk about sarcastic. You've been that way all evening."

'Yeah, I had a good teacher, I just copied you." He said pulling her up out of the chair and kissed her.

"Oh..." She said smiling and remembering how much she had been in love with him.

"Oh, what?"

"Nothing, just Oh. "What are we going to do tomorrow? Are you up for going to the Tate Gallery?" She said changing the subject. "I would like to go to the place where we used to swim too, remember the beach where we could see Logan Rock?"

"Sure, we'll leave early and take a lunch, I don't' want to spend time in a restaurant. Too many people around. I just want to be alone with you, my petal." He laughed as he kissed her again with thoughts about their past relationship and hoped it would endure this time in their lives.

"You haven't called me that in …well, a long time." She smiled.

"Oh, yes, it's all coming back to me" he said with all the memories of her flooding through his mind.

# Chapter Fifteen

Timothy laid awake his first night in Florence.

He couldn't get the pictures of David and Sarah's wedding and the day Karri informed him about her new plans to stay in London to become a veterinarian out of his mind to be able to relax and go to sleep.

His deserted feeling brought on from his children's decision to stay in London leaving him completely alone was unbearable. What was he going to do? How was he to survive without them?

They had been his whole life other than his business but which he wouldn't allow to take over his life so he could spend the time needed with his children, and make sure they had all they needed, not only eating properly, well clothed and doing well in school, but also emotionally. With their mother's premature death resulting from cancer, he knew they would need more from him than a normal father children relationship that included a mother.

Now, unexpectedly they were almost out of his life. He felt isolated. His mourning for his wife hadn't been this painful as he had his children's love to fill part of the loneliness and gave him the reason to work hard to make the best life for them that was possible under the circumstances. Now he could see their need for him had been cathartic.

Now what? He had to make a plan to get through this devastating situation that he'd abruptly found himself in. That was exactly what he would do, make a plan to get his mind off the painful fact he was totally alone for the first time in his life.

The bright Italian sun streaked through the slightly parted curtains in the ornate hotel suite in Florence. The decision to take this trip with Beth had been a rescue from his doldrums and sudden impact of being left alone.

The phone rang and when he tried to reach for it, and inadvertently knocked over the picture in the small brass frame he had at the last moment put in his suitcase that he took of David and Karri just before they left on their trip to London.

"Hello, Beth, sure, I'm just now getting up. I'll be down to meet you."

The dull ache of emptiness was still there.' This will take some time.'He thought as he let the hot shower beat down on him.' It is not going to be an easy task, this letting goes of my children and let them live their own lives. I can't allow them to know this is so hard for me to accept. I will pretend I am happy for them and their choices.'

"Over here, Timothy."

"Sorry I'm late; I just couldn't get to sleep. Guess traveling does that to me did you sleep well?"

"I did, I really crashed."

"What's on the agenda today?"

"Let's start with the art museums and the Palazzo Vecchio. Have you been before/"

"No, just Rome when I was on a university break one summer with my family. I was overwhelmed with all the art."

"You haven't even seen art until you see Florence. This is the place for art study. All the art history books are filled with the art that is housed here. This is my favorite place in Italy. I love Tuscany."

"Are you going to teach?"

"I don't think so, as I said before, I need to be home when the boys come home from school. I don't want to miss anything they might want to share with me from their day.

I remember how I used to love to go home and tell my mother all the things that happened at school. I look back on it now and she must have had a lot of laughs from my days at school and the interesting school friends and what we would do and accomplish in a day.

One day I couldn't wait to tell her about my friend Tommy, who ate the goldfish right out of the goldfish bowl that sat on the teacher's desk. One of the other boys dared him to do it and he did." She laughed.

"You can only hope that Ashton and Brandon won't be the one to eat the fish."

They both laughed at that and shared many other stories about their children and the things they had said and done.

Beth could sense his deep love and now his loneliness for his children and how time passes so quickly before you know it, they are grown.

The day passed quickly. Timothy was amazed with the art that was there. He couldn't imagine the old masters doing such splendid work under such poor circumstances. No running water, no modern conveniences.

The couple decided to eat their evening meal at the open-air café down from the luxurious hotel where they were staying.

The lights in Florence covered the buildings with a warm golden orange hue making sure everyone knew the old master's art was safely nestled in their rightful places and no harm would come to them.

"The air here is so different from London, isn't it? London has such a thick oil and petrol aroma, and here it is more fragrant. Have you noticed?" Beth asked.

"Yes, most definitely. I didn't realize London had a strong petrol smell until I came back this time. That was the first thing David and Karri noticed as well. Funny how things like that don't even come to your attention until you leave and then return."

"I suppose so; I don't ever want to leave my home in London. My whole life has revolved around 'St. John's Glen'. I want my sons to enjoy their lives there the way I did. I want to make wonderful memories for them. I don't want any regrets. I want to smooth over any pain they have concerning their father and his absence in their lives. I don't want that part of their life to become a thorn in their side that they can't heal from as some children from a broken home I have seen when I was a child."

"How long has it been since he left?"

"You mean how long has it been since I finally threw him out?"

"Yes." Anthony smiled.

"Two years. We had our own home that we were going to renovate and buy surrounding land to enlarge our grounds. With his eye for the women, he saw every day at work and at parties and our social life added to his drinking alcohol every day, our marriage didn't stand a chance. I should have thought about his habits when we were going together but, you know the old saying "love is deaf, dumb and blind." It is, I can testify to that, otherwise I would have seen through him. He had such a charming manner I was swept off my feet."

"Sorry about that. You must be still having a hard time overcoming your divorce."

"It's getting better. I still have my bad days, but I try not to allow them to take over my life. I can at least choose not to let it get me down. Thank goodness for the twins, they are my lifesavers."

"I know what you mean, David and Karri were mine too when my wife died. I put everything I had into them. They saved me from wanting to curl up and die with her. We really had a fantastic relationship. She was so warm and giving and sharing. I was amazed at her ability to make everyone who came in contact with her feel good."

"O.K. tomorrow if it's all right with you I want to rent a car and drive around Tuscany. How does that sound?"

"Sounds good to me, I've heard about the countryside and how beautiful it is, so I'm looking forward to it."

# Chapter Sixteen

Elizabeth stretched and yawned feeling good about being back home in her own bed. The trip had been a good one. She and Anthony decided to pursue their relationship and find out if they were meant to be together, which had she had thought from the first day she met him.

After their past failures in relationships the controlled environment she'd lived in with her father and his ex-wife's affairs they wanted to take their time and let things happen naturally and not force anything.

She felt very good about his parents. They were accepting of her and she like them.

Anthony's cousin Nigel, was another matter, what was he going to see her about when he came to London? Anthony warned her he was up to something and to be careful when he came to visit her.

He had to return to Italy and do some business and start painting again. He'd wanted her to go with him but she had her classes that she wanted to take and to continue with the plans she had for the ones she'd signed up for before starting her regular ones at the university next month and there was still the driving. She also opted for a ballroom dancing class and a fencing class. Maybe she would find something else more exciting. She was thirsty for adventure.

After she had her shower, she went downstairs to take a swim before breakfast when she saw Nigel in the entry way. Hodges was almost ready to ring her.

That was quick she thought, when she saw him.

"Miss Elizabeth, you have company a Mr. …"

"Thank you, Hodges. Hello Nigel, this is a surprise. Come have breakfast with me." She said walking out to the pool area, smiling and remembering Anthony's warning.

"Just tea would be fine, I've already had breakfast." He said looking around at the perfect setting. "You have a beautiful estate. I suppose it has been in the family for centuries?"

"Yes, it has."

"So who will your heir be?"

The question made her mad the thought of him being so nosey. "I..."

He interrupted her. "I know it is none of my business, but you need to think about it. Have you checked the trust lately?"

"No, I was going to but I haven't had time."

"Just wanted you to be on top of things. You can't be too careful. When you're gone it's too late."

"I think it's been set up for generations for the oldest son to be heir and it's as simple as that." She said getting angry in his persistence.

"But, now what?"

"None of your business. I'm sorry, but please, it's none of your business."

"All right, I'm sorry, a bad habit I have about trusts that are left unattended. I won't bring it up again, I promise, I just came to see if you would like to go to the theatre? Is there something you'd like to see?"

"Well, let me think, I haven't seen 'Phantom' and I would love to see it. That would be fun. I would enjoy that."

"Wonderful, I will have my secretary call for reservations. Tell me what your schedule is so she can make them when you are free.

"I am free all this week in the evenings, so anytime would be fine."

"Good, that's settled. I have to go to a meeting so I will be in touch when she calls."

"Good bye, Nigel, and thank you and I will be waiting for your call." She said as Hodges escorted him out.

Wondering why he couldn't have just phoned to make the date.

Nigel was two years older than Anthony. He was tall and handsome with large brown eyes that didn't miss anything within his range. His quick wit and charm and his ability to be in control of every situation was an enticement to the women that he would came in contact with. His smile would melt even the coldest of hearts. Nigel couldn't be more different from his cousin.

Anthony was also very handsome; he had blondish hair and large incredible hazel-green eyes. He was very quiet and reserved and was a very a sincere person. He didn't have the charisma with the ladies that Nigel possessed.

He had been very aware as they were growing up how inept he felt around the opposite sex and could never find the words he wanted to say to them. He always felt uncomfortable in their presence. Then he met Elizabeth at university and could converse with her but at the same time had found he could never totally relax when they were together, he was always on edge. With her quick wit and sarcasm, he was never quite sure how to take the things she would say.

Elizabeth was slightly interested in Nigel and did remember the warning from Anthony. She did feel his coming on too strong about the trust. But it had brought the idea of how it was set up now that her father had passed away and she was the heir. Her heir would not be a Rose. So, she thought she would find out from her attorneys what the trust needed now to be updated, and how her heirs if she would ever have any would fit into the Rose Trust for the coming generations.

"I'll have breakfast now. I'm starved." She said to the maid as she removed Nigel's cup and saucer.

Elizabeth dove into the water for her swim while waiting for her meal.

She loved this time of day and this time of year she always felt free as she swam.

Feeling better than she had in years it was invigorating to think maybe Anthony would find out about the date with Nigel. Served him right for running off to the continent so quickly. They'd barely had a week together. This delicious thought made her swim even faster.

Nigel had kept his word. They would be going to see Phantom the next evening. Elizabeth was excited. For the first time in years, she was going to the theater.

She took extreme care as she dressed for the theater and her first date, she'd had other than Anthony in years. It felt good to think about getting back into a societal life.

"Elizabeth, you look radiant. Where have you been all my life?" Nigel asked escorting her to his car.

"I've been here locked in my castle. Now I am free. It feels so good to get out and enjoy life. Thank you for tonight.
"

"You are so welcome. I haven't been to the theater in a long time either. I've been working so much lately I've forgotten how to enjoy life."

"That's sad; you need to get out like I plan to."

"I will, let's do it together, and what do you say?"

"Well, some. I have other matters to attend to. So, we'll see."

"Good enough for me just keep me in mind."

The curtain came down on the stage leaving Elizabeth spell bound. She had been totally engrossed in the play and the music and hadn't realized that Nigel was even there.

"Well, how did you like it?" Nigel asked carefully placing her wrap around her shoulders.

"I was totally there with them. The music carried me away. This was magnificent."

"How would you like to meet some of the actors?"

"Are you kidding me?"

"I wouldn't kid you. "He laughed at her reaction." I'll take you to meet them." As he led her backstage.

"Nigel. Hello, haven't seen you for a while, where have you been?"

"I've been busy with work. It never gets caught up. Lydia, I'd like you to meet Elizabeth Rose, Elizabeth this is Lydia."

"I am so glad to meet you. Your performance tonight was outstanding. You have a beautiful voice."

"Thank you, Elizabeth. I love this play and I never get tired of Christine."

"See you later Nigel, Elizabeth, I have to change. Oh, by the way, there is a party tomorrow night for one of the cast members that is leaving, want to come? If you do, call me and I'll get you on the list. "

"Wonderful, yes, I will be there put me down." He said as he kissed her bye.

"Nigel. Where have you been?" Another cast member asked slapping him on the back.

"Working, really busy working."

"Hi Paul, I want you to meet Elizabeth Rose. She thoroughly enjoyed the play."

"Nice to meet you, Elizabeth."

"Wonderful to meet you. I loved the songs you sang. You have an incredible voice."

"Thank you, the music keeps me interested or I couldn't do this every night. Nice meeting you I have to get out of this make up."

The actors and chorus were very friendly and accommodating. Elizabeth was very impressed with Nigel's close association with them and they all seemed to like him, even the invitation to the cast party.

Nigel walked her to his car and opened the door for her then suddenly before she could sit down, took her in his arms and kissed her.

Elizabeth pulled away from him turning her head away from his.

"All right, I will behave. I promise. I'll take you home."

The drive to Roselyn was quiet. Nigel didn't mention anything about her going with him to the party the next evening and she kept waiting for him to invite her, but no invitation came.

"Well, here we are my lady, thank you for a wonderful evening and we will have to do this again. I'll phone you." He said walking her to the door and waited for Hodges to open it for her.

"Good night, Nigel, and thank you again. I had such an enjoyable evening meeting your friends. They really are talented." She said still waiting for him to invite her to the party the next evening.

"They are gifted and I am fortunate to have them for friends. I'll call you."

He said as he left her at the door and kissed her on the forehead good bye.

Very puzzled at his obvious exclusion to the party the next evening Elizabeth was finding a slight interest in the cousin Anthony warned her about. She couldn't understand why he hadn't invited her to the party?

# Chapter Seventeen

"Under the Tuscan sun. I just can't get over how beautiful it is here. Not only the scenery but all the centuries of art. The museums, statues, and especially the statue of David. I am so glad I came with you Beth. Thank you. This has been great. Timothy said as they sat at the sidewalk café.

"When are you going back to L.A.?"

"I don't know. I want to talk to David and Karri first to make sure they are settled before I leave. I think they are all right but guess it's out of habit."

"I'm sure you will find it completely different when you return. What will you do with all your time?"

"I haven't allowed myself to think about it. I dread that first day back. I know it will be devastatingly lonesome. I will have to get some hobbies. Maybe get into golf or something like my friends. They seem to get absorbed in the game. "

"I've heard that too about golf. I just never had the desire to hit a poor little innocent ball around all over hills and ponds, and never thought that would be fun. It looked boring to me. When the sports announcers on TV that are reporting the game, they whisper. I always wondered why they had to whisper." Beth laughed. "Oh, Isn't that Anthony?" She asked leaning forward to get a better view.

"Anthony? Who's Anthony?"

"He is Elizabeth's friend from school. They met at university years ago. He was going to marry her, but your father told him to get lost, in so many words."

She gave Timothy a quick summary of Elizabeth's long-lost love.

"Anthony, over here." Beth called out to him across the street.

"Beth. What a surprise. What are you doing here?" He asked coming over to their table.

"Anthony, I want you to meet Timothy, Mr. Rose's younger brother, the one that moved to America. Timothy, this is Anthony, Elizabeth's friend from university."

"Hello, glad to meet you, Timothy."

"Nice to meet you as well."

"This is nice, Anthony to see you here. We are going back to London day after tomorrow so it will give us a chance to catch up on the latest. When was the last time you saw Elizabeth?"

"Just three days ago. I took her with me to see my parents in Cornwall. We had a nice visit, but I had to get back here and take care of some things and do some painting. I don't want to get behind. She was a little upset that I had to leave so soon. When you get back smooth it over for me will you?"

"Of course, I will you know I would do anything for both of you. I only hope someday you will finally get together. You can't seem to get on an even keel, can you?"

"That's putting it mildly. We're if anything upside down most of the time and just trying to have a normal conversation is a miracle. "He laughed.

"I know, you have always been that way. I was hoping now that well, since Mr. Rose had passed away things would change for the better, or rather the smoother." She laughed.

"It was touch and go there for a while in Cornwall, but we finally were able to settle down and have some decent discussions with out her making questions out of my statements. She has this unnerving habit of doing that or restating everything I say making fun of me. Does she do that to either of you?" He asked them as they felt his sincerity.

"No, no really, but I haven't had that many conversations with her. Only casual ones usually about the weather and the one night we found Creighton's journals."

"She hasn't done that to me either. I won't let her bully me around. Anthony, you have to stand up to her. Let her know you are not a push over. She doesn't' realize what she is doing most of the time; it really is a game to her. She loves to see people 'stammer and sputter' and she once confided in me years ago."

"Oh, yes she does know what she is doing. She even confessed to me in Cornwall that she had a bad habit of doing that to me and promised she would stop it. So, hope the next time I see her she will remember what she said."

"When are you going back to London, Anthony?"

"Not for a while. I have too much work to do. Wish I could take it with me."

"Why couldn't you paint in London, or Cornwall? Why here?"

"I never thought about it, really, I guess I could, I just get so inspired here and Paris. I suppose it's because the old masters were here and I can feel it so much stronger while I am on the continent."

'Think about it. How are you going to ever going to have a relationship with Elizabeth if you're not around her?"

"I'll try to work things out. You said you were leaving the day after tomorrow?"

"I guess that is the plan. We aren't set in stone. Would it make a difference if we waited for you and we could all go back together?" Timothy asked getting interested in his cousin's personal life and sensing he needed their help with Elizabeth.

"Yes, if I am to get things sorted out, I will need a few days and I would like for you both if you could stay until I do. I need your moral support Beth, as usual. Remember? If it wasn't for you, I wouldn't have gotten through the... well almost engagement thing." Anthony said looking down at the sidewalk.

"Good, that's settled then, we will wait for you and until then we can enjoy some more of this beautiful country. Here's our numbers call when you have some time and we can at least have meals together." Beth said handing him her card.

"Here's my card and my shop is just across the street. It's really small but it is all I need. I have an apartment two blocks down that is good sized for me to entertain when I need to. It's recessed back from the street enough to give privacy and to be able to have a small courtyard in front.

My clients are my social friends too and we give parties once in a while and I needed to have enough room for entertaining. I never thought I would be the entertaining type did you Beth?" He laughed.

"Never in my wildest dreams. You were always the wall flower so to speak."

"I will get back with you as soon as I can." He said shaking hands with Timothy and giving Beth as kiss on the cheek.

"He seems like a very nice guy. I can see him with Elizabeth. They both have innocence about them. I don't mean... Oh, I don't' know, they just seem to go together." Timothy surmised.

"That's an interesting observation, but a correct one. Innocence. For their age you'd think they'd be worldlier, but somehow, they have missed out on life's lessons in treachery and deceit that I was taught by my former husband. I admire that quality in them. You have it too." She observed.

"Me? Oh, you better be careful, I can be very treacherous and deceitful. I'm in imports and exports." He laughed.

"What shall we do today while we wait for Anthony?" She asked.

"Let's drive to Pisa. I want to see the leaning tower."

"Wonderful, me too, I haven't been there for a long time." Beth said as she relaxed in the soft tan leather seat preparing herself for a wonderful ride to one of her favorite cities in Tuscany.

# Chapter Eighteen

Elizabeth sat on her new floral cushioned window seat in her bedroom starring down at the immaculate gardens and perfectly trimmed lush green hedges. She wondered why Nigel hadn't phoned. He was supposed to call her so they could do something together again after their night at Phantom but he hadn't been in touch. She wondered who he took to the cast party that next night when he had been invited by the leading lady in the show.

She had a ball room dancing class in the afternoon and then in the morning she had her first fencing lesson.

When she was growing up her mother thought she needed to have a dance class to help her become graceful and she had quite enjoyed it. When she went to university, she stopped the classes as she felt she'd outgrown it. The lasting effects of those several years in class remained with her and made her into the graceful woman she was that day. Feeling the need to add something with movement in her life besides regular exercise she'd decided on ballroom dancing and fencing.

"Miss Elizabeth, there is a gentleman to see you, he is waiting downstairs in the library. His name is *Nigel* Chadwick." The maid said softly emphasizing the first name.

"Tell him I will be there in just a few minutes." She said quickly changing clothes from her shorts into a casual pale yellow summer frock, and then applied some last-minute lipstick and mascara.

"Hello, Nigel"

"Hello, Elizabeth, you look wonderful as usual."

"Thank you, how have you been?"

"Fine and you?"

"Fine." She said wondering what was up now that the party was over and he hadn't invited her.

"I was wondering if you would like to go dancing tomorrow night. Some of my friends are going out and wanted me to come along. Does that sound good to you?"

"Where would we be going? What club?"

"Oh, not a club, it would be at the Savoy Hotel."

"Really? Well, I suppose so, what time?"

"I will pick you at nine o'clock. "

"It is black tie and formal?"

"Yes, it is."

"All right I will be ready at nine o'clock"

He took her hand and lightly brushed it with a faint kiss and left.

'That was quick.' She thought. 'No interfering conversation just the invitation and he left. What is he up to?' She couldn't help but wonder.' Why didn't he just call? Why come all this way when he could have just phoned?' Anthony's warning still was utmost in her thoughts at that moment. She thought too that 'he was up to something.'

Elizabeth wanted to look especially good for the date with Nigel. Even though she didn't quite understand him and where he was coming from she wanted to look her best.

She decided to go to the spa and then have them come out to do her hair and make-up.

Nigel could not help but stare as he watched Elizabeth gracefully coming down the long staircase. Her hair that was piled high on her head had enhanced her natural beauty and the flawless skin that glowed through her freshly made-up face.

"Elizabeth you are beautiful. I mean you are stunning." He said sincerely as he   cleared his throat.

"Thank you, Nigel, you look quite charming in your tux." She said trying not to let him know how truly nervous she was.

"Your carriage awaits my lady." He said once again carefully placing her wrap around her shoulders as if her were sculpting her.

She could feel her heart pound as he finished with the wrap and then took her arm to take her to the car.

"Do you enjoy dancing?" He asked.

"Yes, I do, as a matter of fact I am taking some ball room dancing. It has been so long since I've danced and it was exhilarating."

"Good, I love it too. It affects me the same way."

"Nigel, so glad you could come. "The beautiful young woman greeted him as they walked into the reserved room at the Savoy.

"Thank you for letting me know you would be here. I want you to meet Elizabeth Rose. Elizabeth this is Cynthia Goodman."

"Nice to meet you" Elizabeth said softly impressed with how beautiful she was.

Nigel led her to the table where the rest of the party was that they were to join.

The music was wonderful. Each melody was inviting. Then a tango started to play and Nigel stood up took her hand and asked her to dance.

"I hope I can remember what to do. I've just had one class. So don't be expecting too much." She said apologetically.

The couple was immersed in the music and when it ended everyone complimented them on their expertise on the floor.

The evening went very well and Elizabeth forgot about Anthony's warning, relaxed, and enjoyed the delight of dancing with Nigel's expert way of leading her around the floor.

The next day she was lying by the pool in the warm July sun where she was still feeling the effects of the night before and found herself humming some of the music that had been played last night when she and Nigel had danced.

She was wondering about the curious call from Beth, that she and Timothy would be there today and for her to be sure to be at home so they could see her as they had a very special gift for her that they'd found in Tuscany.

Elizabeth was very pleased with the relationship that they had formed and her intuition was correct when her best friend and uncle first met and she had felt their chemistry. 'Wouldn't that be something if they were serious?' She thought.

The day grew to an end but no sign of Beth or Timothy. She decided to shower and put on a cool dress and go back outside and read.

Cranston had some ideas for some new plants around the pool and before he would put them in the permanent heavy urns and vases, he had them in the ones with wheels so she could wheel them around to her satisfaction and she could arrange them the way she wanted and not have to try to push the heavy pots.

The gentle summer breeze gently made its way through the courtyard not only making a faint rustling noise and adding ripples in the turquoise blue water in the pool but also filling the area with sweet fragrances of diverse flora and fauna. The soft glow of carefully placed lanterns highlighted the perfect scene and made an exquisite haven to all those who entered.

"Miss Elizabeth, Mr. Chadwick is here, uh... Mr. Nigel Chadwick that is. He would like to speak to you, is it all right if I bring him out here to see you?" Hodges asked.

"Yes, that would be fine."

"Hello, Elizabeth how are you?"

"I am fine, and you?"

I am fine as well. I just wanted to see how you were doing and find out when we could get together for our 'fencing 'date?"

"I forgot about that. Let me see, I don't have another driving lesson for another week, I can't do that but every so often I get so nervous when I'm in the car.     Travis makes it look so easy, but there are so many things you have to do and think about when you're sitting in the driver's seat." She laughed. "So how about tomorrow? I have one planned at 2 o'clock?"

"Good, it will give me a chance to touch base with a client I'm working with. I could pick you up here about, half past one?"

"Would you like something to eat or drink?" She asked as he sat down.

"A cold drink would be great."

Elizabeth rang Bea to bring a pitcher of lemonade.

Bea placed the bright orange tablecloth on the white wrought iron table with the large pitcher, while the music from the courtyard speakers played softly in the background.

"This is nice." He said taking a sip from the frosted glass and relaxed in his chair facing Elizabeth. "I suppose you have been wondering why I've been around so much lately?"

"As a matter of fact, I have. So out with it, I am curious."

"Well, when I first began visiting with you it was for a lark. I wanted to see if I could make ole' Anthony jealous. Then I found I liked you. I enjoyed our times together. So now that everything is out in the open, do you suppose we could pursue a relationship?"

"What do you mean a relationship?"

"Well, you know, a…well, romance?"

Elizabeth sat frozen in her chair not able to move or speak. She was caught so completely off guard with his intimate and straightforward question she could not find the words to reply.

"I'm sorry to startle you, but I have had such a run of bad luck with the ladies in the past I don't want to get off on the wrong foot with you. I would like to have a relationship built on truth and trust. I have not always been able to do that in the past. Some of it was my fault and some of it derived from my ex-wives. Anyway, I have finally grown up want a solid future. One where my next wife and I will have an open dialogue no secrets, no deceit."

"Nigel, this is not at all what I had thought our relationship would turn into. I only wanted a friend. Someone to do things with. I have truly enjoyed my time with you as well, but you must know now I am…well…I have to tell you that…"

"You're in love with that bone head Anthony?" He tried to laugh'

"Yes." She said softly looking into his eyes, where she tried to prevent tears from forming in hers but failed.

Handing her his handkerchief he continued as she dabbed at the sudden tears.

"Sorry, I didn't mean to make you cry." He said softly. "Why haven't you two gotten together sooner?"

"My father told him to not to come around anymore. So, he didn't. He went to Paris and Italy and Alicia's wedding was the first time I'd seen him in years. I'd heard he'd married and so I thought well that's that then. Now that he is divorced, I thought maybe we could make it work this time. Now I don't know. He left a couple of weeks ago and I haven't heard from him since we were in Cornwall."

"That jug head, he doesn't deserve you. He hasn't called once?"

"No, he hasn't. I don't know what he's doing."

"Well, I hope you know what you are doing, he is a very closed person you know. His ex-wife used to complain about this to me. She never knew what he was thinking. He wouldn't or couldn't share his thoughts with her."

"Is that why she had affairs?" Elizabeth replied curtly in Anthony's defense.

"Ooo...you are on his side, aren't you?"

"I am on his side and always will be. I understand him well enough to know if his 'ex 'had any real intent of making their marriage work with him they would have found a way. But you can't make anything work built on lies."

"I guess so, I suppose I didn't know her well enough, did I?"

"No, and you don't know your cousin well enough either."

"So, now does this mean we are still on for fencing? Or am I cast out now that I have confessed my evil plan?"

"I don't think so, I mean, I don't want to pursue anything with you any further. I am glad we had this talk though. I thank you for your honesty but I want to wait for Anthony and see if we have a future." She said getting up from her chair to escort him to the front door where Hodges was standing by to open the door for him.

"Goodnight, Nigel."

"Goodnight Elizabeth." He said looking back over his shoulder for one last look at the person he thought he might have had a chance to make a solid future.

# Chapter Nineteen

The music stopped and Anthony released Beth from his tight grip. She had suggested he needed to practice dancing to be able to compete with Nigel.

Elizabeth had kept her informed of their date at the Savoy and that they had plans to attend the fencing class together.

Timothy would help him with fencing. His extracurricular activity at university had been filled with the fencing club as well as others and was willing to share with his cousin's friend his expertise.

The couple wanted to see Anthony confident when he saw her again before he let her know he had returned from Italy.

The trio had formed a friendship in Tuscany where Beth wanted to once again help her friend be successful and confident when he could find the courage to purpose to Elizabeth and have him up on his dancing and allow Timothy to teach him how to fence. These two things could add to his confidence and help him and Elizabeth have even more in common.

"I need to phone Elizabeth and tell her when to expect a visit from you. Should I phone her now?" Beth asked as they all three sat down on the large white leather circular sofa resting against the light teak wooden wall in her family room.

"Yes, I guess I need to phone her.

You know, I always wanted just a nice simple quite girl to marry and settle down with and have children. Then I met Elizabeth and she was so sarcastic and witty and funny, and fell in love with her so by the time I thought well, I could handle that her father told me to buzz off, so I did as I was told, ending that possibility of a life with her.

Then I made great the mistake of marrying an Italian siren, and found she chased everything in pants not skipping a beat when we got married. So, now I am further back on the path of romance path than ever, and getting older by the minute." He sighed with the mini capsule of his romantic life that had been such a failure.

"Sorry, Anthony, and I can empathize with you, my 'ex' also had affairs. I didn't even bother to count them. I just knew there were several. Finally, I could not endure it any longer even for the twin's sake. I thought at first he would grow up, but he only got worse."

"That is so sad and how ironic is this? My wife and I had a wonderful marriage. She was loving and faithful to the children and me. We had such wonderful plans for our future. We even wanted more children. Then we were told one day she had cancer and a year later she was gone. My life ended. If it had not been for David and Karri, I wouldn't have made it. Compared to both your experiences in marriage mine was the best and yet she died.

When my parents died shortly after she died, David, Karri, and I moved to America, mainly because I wanted to get away from Creighton. Now I find he had good reason to hate me the way he did. Too bad I had not been aware of what he was going through so I might have helped him and we could have at least had a tolerable relationship. Guess it was not to be though. When you look back over your life it comes to your things work out the way they do for the best. Don't you think?"

Timothy asked as he too shared a short synopsis of his life.

"I suppose so, life turns out the way it must have been designed. I don't have any other way of looking at it. We plan and plan and yet something out of our control smashes it to bits. So guess I'm glad to have this second chance to sweep my beautiful one with the acid tongue back into my life this time forever.....I hope." Anthony sighed as he phoned Elizabeth to let her know he was back and wanted to see her.

The three laughed at his last remarks hoping their latest endeavors would pay off and that there would be a wedding in the near future for the ill-fated pair.

"Is this my little petal?" Anthony asked tauntingly and winking at Beth and Timothy.

"I …well... yes." she said playing along with him wanting to see where he was and what he was doing.

"I wanted to come over and see you. I can be there shortly if you are going to be home."

"I will be home and do, come over."

"That went smooth; I hope that is the indicator of how the rest of it will go." Anthony said as he was walking to his rented car.

"I am sure the worst is over and you both will be able to get on the right path and get on with your well-deserved life together." Beth said as she kissed him good-bye.

"Well, that's that. Now…what about us? "Timothy asked as he put his arm around Beth's shoulder looking down into her clear blue eyes.

"What about us? That could mean many things. It could mean well, here we are, we could have dinner, we could take the boys to a movie, we could…."

Timothy kissed her before she could say anything else.

"You know exactly what I mean. What about us?" He asked as they walked through the large house to the pool area where they sat down at one of the tables.

"I don't know how we could ever have a long-distance relationship. They don't work I've had friends that tried but they never lasted."

"I was thinking about opening another business in London. I had one here once before and it was doing well when I moved to California. I am sure I can do the same here. I want to keep the one there so my friends can keep working for me and not interrupt their lives closing the business. They have done such a wonderful job of running everything while I've been gone, I know they would continue that way if I moved back here." He said watching her reaction to his new idea.

"That would be nice. We would see how things might work out?"

"What do you mean might."

"We aren't kids any longer. I know my feelings for you; tell me how you feel about me." He asked looking straight into her eyes this time searching for the truth, how she felt about him.

"You tell me first how deep your feelings towards me are." She asked stalling.

"I love you, Beth." He said simply taking her hand in his. I think the first time I saw you at Roselyn, I loved you. "

"Well, when you stepped out of the swimming pool at Roselyn, I knew by my racing heart you could be the one for me. I had to see if you were as good a man as I had guessed that first day. That's why I came up with the Tuscany trip." She confided.

"Well, I am surprised; I just thought you needed a traveling companion to brush up on your art classes."

"Well, in a way that was true, but the real test for me with people is to travel with them. You can learn so much about a person on a trip especially an extended one like the one we took. You were so easy going. You didn't' get upset when orders weren't as you'd ordered, everything, you were so calm and easy to be around, but the big test was observing you when the beautiful girls would walk by and you didn't go out of your way to take a second or third look as my husband used to. I remember even now when we were just going together, he did that, I should have caught on then what life would be like after marriage. You were so…well…so …."

"You're trying to say I'm easy?" He laughed at her summary of him.

"Yes, that is exactly what I am trying to say. You are easy Mr. Timothy Rose, I love you." She said before she could stop the heartfelt words from slipping out.

"That's the word I was afraid to say before I knew how for sure how you felt about me, yes, I love you too and I have been so surprised it happened so quickly and …. Yes, so easily." He said coming over to her chair as she raised up reaching for him to take her in his arms.

"I wonder what Elizabeth is going to say about us? She is so opinionated I hope we can withstand whatever she will have to say. "Beth sighed snuggling deeper into his embrace for reassurance and protection from whatever his niece would have to say about this new and surprising turn of events.

# *Chapter Twenty*

After hanging up from Anthony's call telling her he was on his way to see her Elizabeth   hurriedly reached for her favorite blue summer dress in the white louvered door closet that was   just added to her room. Excitedly she threw it on the bed and ran into the bathroom grabbed her toothbrush with one hand and her hairbrush with the other.

Peering at her reflection in the large gold trimmed mirror she observed how pretty she looked as her eyes shined with great expectations of Anthony's highly anticipated and welcomed visit.

Running back out to the bed she snatched the dress up and slid it quickly over her head and returned to the brightly lit bathroom where she carefully but hurriedly applied a touch of make up wanting to look her best for him.

"Miss Elizabeth, *Anthony* Chadwick is here to see you." This time emphasizing Anthony.

"Take him to the courtyard and seat him by the pool. Tell him I will be there in just a few minutes. Oh, ask him if he wants something to drink. Or eat or both."

She said getting out of breath.

Anthony sat watching the faint ripples in the pool. The sunlight emphasized the blue color of the water giving the courtyard an oasis feeling.

He took a deep breath and listened to the music that added a romantic mood to the picture-perfect scene.

"Elizabeth wanted to know if you would like to have something to eat and drink. She will be here in just a few minutes." Bea said as she put a fresh white tablecloth on the table.

"Just a cold drink, maybe Mrs. Waverly's lemonade?" He asked.

He tried to relax in the cushioned chair, he wanted to get this day over and done with. After rehearsing it so many times, he was just tired of anticipating Elizabeth's sarcastic remarks and making questions out of his statements as she usually did and only wanted to get it all over with.

He had wondered so many times if this was all worth it. Why didn't he just tell her off and never come back. However, he knew in his heart why he could not leave and forget the whole Rose episode.

She was the only one who could make him so mad he could scream when they were together and usually did silently, yet she was the only one he loved deeply enough that made his heart mourn in her absence.

The shallowness of his love for his ex-wife in addition to her unfaithfulness made it impossible for them to work things out even though she had asked for forgiveness and wanted a second chance.

"Anthony, I am so glad to see you. Are you here to stay for a while?" She asked noticing her heart was thumping so loud she hoped she could hear his reply.

"We'll see, I'm not sure, depends on how things work out."

"I am happy you are here, we, that is David, Sarah and Karri are having a birthday party for Timothy Saturday night. Will you be able to come?"

"Sure, what time?"

"You could come anytime; the party will start at eight o'clock. He doesn't know we are doing this; we have one huge surprise for him  and we can't wait to see his face when we give it to him."

"I have to wait as well to find out what it is?"

"Yes, no one knows but me David and Alicia."

"Now that is out of the way, I wanted to talk to you..."

"Sorry, hello, Alicia, yes, we have it all under control, I am so glad you are back, Anthony is here you want to come over and have lunch with us? Let me check first, can you stay for lunch?" She asked Anthony.

"Yes." He nodded getting agitated not able to get her attention. Her chatter was adding to the anxiety of why he had come back from Italy and why he was with her at that moment. He watched her radiant face as she finally concluded her call from her sister. He did love her and wanted to get their life started. He was tired of being alone and tired of the years of stressful feelings about her. He just wanted to be calm and live a serene life with her for the rest of his life, with no    concerns about infidelity and erratic communication.

"Sorry about that. Now tell me what you have been doing? Any special projects coming up? I haven't told you in so long how much I love your art."

He stood up and went over to her chair raised her up to him and then asked.
Thank you, I happy you enjoy my art, now, do you love me?"
He asked holding her so close she could not possibly move.

"Love you? Of course, you ninny, I have always loved you. I thought you knew that?"

"How was I supposed to know? You never indicated once that you did. When did I overlook it where were you hiding it, or when did you show it?" He asked starring into her eyes for her answer.

"I don't know, it was just there all along. Couldn't you tell?"

"Not really, maybe once in a while."

"What about when I'd say "you knocked my socks off with that kiss?" She laughed trying to get her breath.

"Well, was that all?" He said holding her even tighter.

"Was that all? You simpleton. Couldn't you feel my love when we were together?"

"Simpleton? What does that mean simpleton? Are you trying to make a point with that brilliant statement?" He laughed at himself reversing the prattle twist she always did with him, still holding her as close as he could.

"You're just trying to wind my up, aren't you? "She laughed searching his eyes to see if he was serious or just teasing her.

"No, I *once and for all want to have a tender conversation* with you without you blasting me with that damned thing you do, with the questions out of what I just said. I don't want to ever go through that again, ok?"

"O.K. I promise, I will try as hard as I cannot ever do that again to you. I don't' know if I can stop cold turkey though." She laughed as she kissed him.

"As long as you at least try to stop it now, at least with me." He said as he kissed her.

They stood starring at each other, absorbing the moment searching for the reality in their relationship and where it was going at that moment.

"What do you think? Will you marry me?"

"What....." She instantly stopped talking before she broke her promise to stop the habit she was trying to break.

"You almost did it again, didn't you?" he laughed.

"Almost, but you see I did stop didn't I?"

"You did, and I am so proud of you, I knew you could do it. See all you have to do is remember." He kept his gaze locked in her eyes.

"Now, I asked you a question, I'm waiting for an answer and I'm not letting you go until you say yes, just the plain yes, not a question, no twist and no twaddle."

"Well...." She stopped again catching herself one more time in her routine of sarcastic remarks and questions. "Twaddle?" She burst out laughing.

"Ah. Elizabeth, you did it again. What am I going to do with you?" He let her go and threw up his arms and stomped his foot.

"I'm sorry, I'm sorry. I did not mean to do that, it just had to come out. I need your help, your patience. I know I can do it, but it's not going to be as easy as I thought is was going to be, please be patient and always remember I am trying to stop, but I can't just quit as fast as I thought I could. Help me?"

"Yes, I will help you and I will try to be patient with you. It's hard to be a big girl and talk nicely, isn't it?" He laughed.

"It is really is hard to just answer the question without at least one remark. It's like I have to say something after someone else does, why do I do that?"

"I don't know, maybe you have to have the last word, there is definitely a psychological issue here, but I sure hope this is the beginning of the end."

"Me too. I'm really sorry, I knew I did this but I didn't realize I couldn't stop doing it so easily, but since I do know this is a real problem I am going to stop, well at least with you."

'Well, when are you going to give me the simple yes answer?"

"Simply yes. I mean yes, just well and simple. Or simply and well. Ah., yes, period end." She stammered laughing at herself.

"We are going to have to prepare ourselves to live finding word stoppers. Phrase catchers, sentence 'enders ', we will have to practice together every day in a role play to get this to end, aren't we?"

"Aren't we......" She stopped and started laughing.

"You will drive me crazy but suppose you can't do it by yourself. Right?"

"What do I say now? Do I say right also? Or do I just nod my head?"

*"Hey that's it. Just nod your head and shut your mouth.* That is how we will do this; I mean stop your madness. You simply... Don't you dare say simply...just nod your head and shut your mouth.  O.K?"

She just looked him in the eye and quietly nodded her head, trying not to laugh, trying not to say one word.

"O.K. but I have to tell you something, but please promise me you won't get mad at me?"

"Mad at you for what?"

Oh, you are *so cute* when you get mad at me it will be so hard not to be able to watch your cute reaction ever again."

"You'll think cute." He said holding her so tight she could not move.

"Maybe I can come up with something else to get that look, do you suppose?"

He looked down into her beaming face and shinning eyes full of mischief and said" I'm sure you'll come up with something."

"Are we going to announce our engagement at the birthday party?" He asked still holding her close.

"Yes."

"Does this mean you are happy to announce it then or wait?"

"Yes. No."

"What does that mean?"

"You asked me if I was happy to announce it then and I said yes to that, then the next question was or wait and my answer to that was no."

"Oh, you did so good my little petal. Very good. I see what you mean now. I have to get used to this so I don't get confused by these simple answers."

He chuckled.

There was not one word from Elizabeth only her thoughts. She just grinned and kept her focus as she searched his all-encompassing hazel green eyes  to make sure  she could prevent herself from saying the word 'simple' and ruin that wonderful romantic moment.

# Chapter Twenty-One

Elizabeth felt her life had come to its fruition that evening from the growing thoughts that had been planted by Nigel's question about her heirs a few weeks earlier which by now had harvested the crop it had yielded from the tiling of the soil of her mind

'This is a very exciting evening for me.' She wrote in her well-worn tan leather diary. '... and I hope for all of us the past and the future globes of the Rose family and that this will make everyone happy.'

With the help from David and Karri, they were planning to unveil, later that night at Timothy's birthday party, a new direction for them all.

'I feel very satisfied and comfortable with the decision I've made about the Rose Family Trust, and I was caught off guard when it came into my mind, but I know this is the right thing to do and I am totally convinced this has to be done. I know life takes dips and turns we don't always see why or where they come from but they do happen and it makes me feel so happy to be part of this monumental twist in mine, and I am convinced a destined one.'

She thoughtfully closed her worn tan leather diary smiling thinking about the reaction she would get from other members of the family. She and Alicia had carefully thought this through and both had come to the same obvious conclusion. That also made her happy to know she was not alone in this decision and her sister had come through and supported her in this decision.

Roselyn glowed for the first time in many years. The radiance from the new indoor and outdoor lighting was only part of it.

Elizabeth was stunning in her white ball gown bought especially for the occasion. She, Alicia, Karri, and Sarah had gone shopping and decided to all buy different shades of white dresses to let everyone know they were related and in the Rose family. They were all radiant that night.

When Anthony saw Elizabeth float down the stairs, he swallowed hard not to allow his throat to go dry. He did not want her to know her effect on him because he thought she would make fun of him, so he did everything he could to remain calm and assured.

He just had his new painting of her hung up in the library and surprise her later on when they could be alone and to be able to share his love for her and his love for her that had gone into his painting, this had been his project for the past several weeks. He'd saved all the pictures he had from their university years and the ones he took of her at Alicia's wedding in the pink flowing chiffon dress that he'd seen her in for the first time in several years that made his heart come alive.

He had arranged an arsenal of photos in his studio in Paris and Tuscany so he could try to get the best painting of her that would endure for the rest of their lives and they would both be proud of. He always thought of her as his pink rose with the thorny stem, which had been why he'd called her petal for short. Then when he had seen her in the pink dress at Alicia's wedding, he knew he had to paint her picture in that dress. It all came together for him in the large portrait of her standing regally in that pink gown, his pink rose.

"Hello, where have you been all my life?" He asked her as he took her hand.

"Right here, under your very nose." She laughed.

"Remember our little deal about you just nod and keep your mouth closed?" He smiled broadly peering into her eyes.

"I remember, I just hope I can keep it up all evening. It will be hard you know, for I love to do that to you and I told you why. So, you may have to go with me everywhere and keep your hand over my mouth."

"I can do that and I will if I have to, so don't get too smart about it."

"I won't, I will try my best to behave myself and nod and keep my mouth shut."

They both laughed as they walked to the kitchen to see if Mrs. Waverly's helpers were following her orders.

"Mrs. Waverly, how is everything going? Do we have everything as planned?"

"Yes, surprisingly we do. The cake is already on the pedestal too. I am very pleased with all the work everyone has done to make this an evening we will never forget."

"More than you know, more than anyone knows." Elizabeth said to herself.

"Is this concerning the big surprise for Timothy?"

"Yes." She smiled and rolled her eyes not to say more.

"Anthony, I need to talk to you about something."

197

"Let's go outside. What's up?" He asked walking her out to the festive courtyard, arrayed in pastel-colored lanterns, and flowers on lily pads holding candles in the center floating on the water adding even more grace and beauty.

"Where will we live after we are married?" Elizabeth asked curiously.

"I have two large apartments' one in Paris and the other one in Tuscany. You can redecorate them any way you want.
"

"Or we could buy something couldn't we? I mean of our own?" She asked.

"Of course, whatever you want to do just so you are there in them oh I forgot about the one in Cornwall, I have a cottage in St. Ives as well. I just bought it last year. I haven't even lived in it yet."

"That is great, so we won't be homeless." She laughed.

"What's this all about?"

"I'll tell you later when the time is right. Oh, there's the birthday boy, you keep him company and busy and don't let him know this is for him remember?'

she reminded him as she hurried away to find David and Karri.

"Got it. Hi Timothy, good to see you again, where's Beth?"

"She is in the powder room; she'll be out in a minute. This is some party."

"It is, how about something to drink?" Anthony asked as he took him by the arm to keep him occupied until he could know the party was for him.

"I wanted to thank you for Tuscany and talking me into coming back for Elizabeth. I know this is the right decision. I just did not want to put up with her little games but I think we are going to be able to conquer it together. I've decided I'm just going to keep my hand over her mouth." He laughed.

"Good luck with that. Have you seen David and Karri?"

"No, I just got here."

"I wanted to tell them about Beth and I and our new plans... I am going to open a new business in London and live here than the ones in California can keep that one going. She wants me to live with her and the twins at St.John's Glen so they can grow up where she did. I do not have a problem with it. It doesn't' matter to me where I live just so I'm with her."

"I know what you mean, I said that same thing to Elizabeth."

"You did purpose then?"

"I sure did and she said a simple yes." He laughed remembering all they went through that night with the routine of breaking her annoying banter habit.

"I really like her and Alicia, I don't know how they turned out so well and normal after having the father they grew up with. Suppose it's in the genes." He smiled.

"I know, you missed the last few years he got even worse as he got older and his illness worsened. I do not know how they survived, especially Elizabeth. Alicia had Jordon." Anthony said sadly thinking about his love camouflaging her sadness with the frustrating word games. "There's my cousin, Nigel, wonder what he's doing here?"

"Nigel, over here. "Anthony called to him.

"Hi, Anthony, how are you?" Nigel sneered…

"I'm doing great, Elizabeth and I are engaged." Anthony bragged.

"Are you kidding me? She must be desperate, 'Priscilla.'" Nigel laughed.

"What did you say?" Anthony asked grabbing him by the collar and lifting him off the floor.

"You heard me, Priscilla."

"I told you to never call me that again and I meant it." Anthony shouted as he punched Nigel in the face, and blood from his nose spurted onto Anthony's new black tux.

"Hold on you two. What's going on here?" Timothy yelled for them to stop, helping Nigel up off the floor.

"Sorry, but that loud mouthed cretin won't let well enough alone. He has to stir things up every time I'm around him."

"What's going on here?" Elizabeth asked as she ran out to see what the shouting was all about.

"Nothing, I just put Nigel in his place where he belongs, under my feet." Anthony smiled reaching for his handkerchief to wipe his hands where his cousin's blood was smeared.

"Are you all right, Tony?" Elizabeth asked as she put her arms around him.

"I'm O.K."

"Let's go into the house, I want to clean you up, you look awful."

"Awful? What do you mean awful?"

"Now you are beginning to sound like me, or well, the old me." She laughed hugging him.

Timothy silently but sternly, escorted Nigel to the front door where Hodges opened it for him to leave and never return as Anthony's future uncle had commanded.

The large old ballroom had been transformed into a dining room for the evening seating each of the 100 guests.

The glittering chandelier radiated its beauty onto the long rows of tables clothed in the Rose family linen cloths, silver, crystal, china and adding to its perfection of pink roses designed into neatly shaped garlands.

Anthony walked with Elizabeth to the ballroom pausing for a moment, before it was time to be seated.

"Thank you for not making more out of this than was necessary. I feel like a third grader coming home school after a fight on the playground. Nigel cannot let me alone. He has to stir things up; he has always been that way from our childhood."

"I think he's jealous of you and can't stand it when you have something you have that he doesn't.....I mean..." She stopped short of revealing Nigel's attempt to share his feelings for her.

"What do you mean has something he doesn't....ah, he *did* come onto you didn't he? That pelic, that...."

"Yes, he did, but I made him leave. I do not know what he was doing here tonight, I did not invite him. He just crashed our party." She said just realizing he came on his own. "

"Sounds like him."

"By the way someone told me Nigel called you 'Priscilla', what was that all about?"

"Great, now I have to go into that. O.K., when I first started to paint mum did not want me to get paint on my clothes so she made me wear her 'penny', her apron. Nigel saw me one day painting in it and made this big issue out of it to everyone he saw after that. I immediately had her make me a painter's smock. A black one." He laughed hugging her and waited for her reaction dreading what it might be.

"That Nigel, you must have had some bad days with him, but I think you must have been so cute in your mum's 'penny'. Now before you get angry at me let me tell you how much I love you and to me everything you do is so cute, sweet and wonderful. You have the best sense of humor; you have proven that putting up with me. You are the most handsome man I have ever known, you are not perfect, but in my eyes you are. I wouldn't trade you for a ....well, a barrel full of monkeys." She laughed kissing him.

"Thank you for allowing me to get that off my chest and come clean with just one of the horrible times I went through with that Nigel. Someday I will tell you more when

I think you are up to it." He chuckled looking down into her beaming face.

"Oh, I can't wait, I will be up to it soon, and, I'm sure."

"Not until after our honeymoon, then if you can be a good girl some rainy day when we are old and bored, I will make you laugh at me some more."

"Bored, how could I ever be bored with you...does this mean until the 12th of never you'll tell me all?" She enjoyed putting him on the spot.

"That's right, until the 12th of Never, and that's a long, long time."

"You should have been a poet, no, I wouldn't change one thing about you, but I sure am sorry I missed seeing you in that 'penny'. "She teased him taking him by the arm and ushering him into the ballroom.

"Mrs. Waverly, please have Hodges announce dinner will be served. Everything is ready?"

"Yes, Miss Elizabeth everything is ready and waiting. You; look beautiful tonight, I have never seen you so beautiful, it has to be Mr. Anthony, he is good for you, isn't he?" She asked winking at him.

"He *is* good for me we are getting married you know."

"No, I didn't know that, we must have an engagement party."

"That sounds good, but it has to be soon, I am not waiting much longer to make her Mrs. Chadwick, Mrs. Anthony Chadwick that is," He announced to make sure everyone would know she was to be *his* wife and *not* his cousin's.

"You just tell me when." She said leaving them to attend to the kitchen and service that was about to begin.

Delightful sounds of cheerful conversation and laughter embellished the carefully decorated room. It had come alive for the first time in many years. The warmth of reuniting old family and friends brought a crescendo to the evening's surprises. Not only the birthday surprise for Timothy, but Elizabeth's grand announcement and the pinnacle moment would be Anthony's first showing of her painting in the rose gown, he had so carefully been working on for the past month.

Elizabeth stood up from her chair, held her glass and tapped it with a knife to get the attention of everyone there to make the surprise for her uncle.

"Good evening, everyone, family and friends. I am so glad you could all be here for this special night. It has been quite an evening so far and will be full of surprises in a few moments. It has been quite a life. I feel very content and happy tonight. Alicia, please come stand with me as I announce that tonight, this is not just a party. Timothy, will you come stand by me as well? "Alicia and Timothy stood on either side of her.

She continued. "Bring the cake in please" she said clapping her hands as they rolled the huge flaming cake to them. "Happy Birthday Timothy." She cried. "Let's toast my father's younger brother on this night. We wish you the best life in the future. We hope from now on your life will be brighter and happier. To you my very young uncle, here's to you." She said as they all raised their glasses and drank to him.

"Speech, speech." David yelled as they all sat down leaving him standing alone.

"This has been quite a surprise. I had no idea there would be a party for me tonight. I am grateful for this chance to thank Elizabeth and Alicia for making this trip one I will never forget. I was simply going to show my children, David and Karri their birth place and let them get a taste of British life. Guess only the taste wasn't enough, they are going to stay here and go to Cambridge. David is entering the International Law School, and Karri is preparing for Veterinary courses. I suppose it had to be this way as I look back over my life growing up here and loving it here at Roselyn. I am happy now they wanted to stay; it is the natural thing to do. Life brings us to full circle, doesn't it? I must say, it also has for me, I shall be staying as well, and will be happy to talk about that later, but tonight I just want to enjoy the night and reconnect with friends and family I have lost contact with over the years. I just want to say thank you for coming and you did make it a wonderful night." He said sitting down.

The guest enjoyed the cake and extended invitations to each other to meet again soon.

Elizabeth rose once again from her chair again tapping on the glass.

"Now that we have celebrated Timothy's birthday, I want to have David and Karri come stand by me." She said embracing them." We have been also been planning another surprise for everyone to hear, I want David to announce this one." She said leaving the brother and sister standing alone.

"I was overwhelmed to say the least when Elizabeth came to me after Sarah returned from our honeymoon with this landmark idea. This milestone in our life. I did not realize anyone could be so generous, thoughtful, kind, loving, caring and sharing as Elizabeth is. I have never nor do I expect to ever know anyone like her again, in my lifetime. I have to publicly thank her and let you all know her grand gesture will affect the rest of our Rose descendants. I am actually still stunned with the fact that she has graciously turned the family trust legally over to me. She told me that since her father did not have sons, she felt very strongly it should go to me. Of course, Karri is included, if something should happen to me before I have heirs, the trust will go to her.

Alicia did not want any part of the trust, as she and Jordan are heirs to his legacy.

We are all very sorry my father and her father were at odds with each other all their lives as you all know. We had a very enlightening evening reading Uncle Creighton's journals. You may not have known their parents were partial to my father, which up to that night he had not been aware.

We have had such an incredible trip to say the least. We were only coming as father said previously to see our birthplace. We were blessed with this new turn of events that has been overwhelming to say the least. I still have not absorbed it all. The main objective of my words tonight is to thank Elizabeth and let her know what an incredible person she it. I am amazed how she not only survived her sad and lonely life but came out of it with sterling character.

This is a night for many surprises, Elizabeth, you have given us ours, now, it's our turn to give you yours.

I hope you will forgive me but I did share my gift from you with Anthony, he called be the next day and asked if he could give you something he wanted to work on. I thought it would be a grand conclusion to our delightful evening.

Hodges, will you bring it in?"

Anthony and Hodges brought the large draped object in and placed it behind Elizabeth.

David continued "Please stand and raise your glasses for one more toast "

As they held their glasses in the air everyone gasped as they starred at the mammoth portrait of her dressed in the pink gown, she wore at Alicia's wedding was unveiled.

"I want to make a toast to… my aunt Elizabeth…. Here's to Elizabeth…. last of the English Roses."

Everyone stood and shouted repeating his words…

"Here's to Elizabeth…last of the English Roses."

# THE END

www.ingramcontent.com/pod-product-compliance
Lightning Source LLC
Chambersburg PA
CBHW020451130626
46549CB00001B/373

# LA ÚLTIMA ILUSIÓN

## Izek Aliev

ARPress

**ARPress**
45 Dan Road Suite 5
Canton MA 02021

Línea directa: 1(888) 821-0229
Fax: 1(508) 545-7580


Información de pedidos:

Ventas en cantidad. Se ofrecen descuentos especiales en compras al por mayor por parte de corporaciones, asociaciones y otros. Para obtener detalles, comuníquese con el editor en la dirección indicada anteriormente.


Impreso en los Estados Unidos de América.

ISBN-13:     Tapa blanda     979-8-89330-914-0
             eBook           979-8-89330-913-3

Número de control de la Biblioteca del Congreso: 2024902694

# CONTENTS

Prologo.................................................................................I
Capítulo 1 ......................................................................... 1
Capítulo 2 ....................................................................... 6
Capítulo 3 ....................................................................... 16
Capítulo 4 ....................................................................... 22
Capítulo 5 ....................................................................... 36
Capítulo 6 ....................................................................... 42
Capítulo 7 ....................................................................... 48
Capítulo 8 ....................................................................... 58
Capítulo 9 ....................................................................... 76
Capítulo 10 ..................................................................... 96
Capítulo 11 ..................................................................... 101
Capítulo 12 ..................................................................... 110
Capítulo 13 ..................................................................... 116
Capítulo 14 ..................................................................... 125
Capítulo 15 ..................................................................... 129
Capítulo 16 ..................................................................... 137
Capítulo 17 ..................................................................... 143
Capítulo 18 ..................................................................... 156
Capítulo 19 ..................................................................... 162
Capítulo 20 ..................................................................... 166
Capítulo 21 ..................................................................... 171
Capitulo 22 ..................................................................... 176
Capítulo 23 ..................................................................... 189
Capítulo 24 ..................................................................... 193
Capítulo 25 ..................................................................... 206